PASSIONATE
PEOPLE
PRODUCE

Copyright © 1997, 2005 by Charles Kovess

Published and distributed in the United States by: Hay House, Inc.,
P.O. Box 5100, Carlsbad, CA 92018-5100 • *Phone:* (760) 431-7695
or (800) 654-5126 • *Fax:* (760) 431-6948 or (800) 650-5115 •
www.hayhouse.com • **Published and distributed in Australia by:**
Hay House Australia Pty. Ltd., 18/36 Ralph St., Alexandria NSW 2015
• *Phone:* 612-9669-4299 • *Fax:* 612-9669-4144 • www.hayhouse.com.au
• **Published and distributed in the United Kingdom by:** Hay House UK, Ltd.
• Unit 62, Canalot Studios • 222 Kensal Rd., London W10 5BN •
Phone: 44-20-8962-1230 • *Fax:* 44-20-8962-1239 • www.hayhouse.co.uk
• **Published and distributed in the Republic of South Africa by:** Hay House
SA (Pty), Ltd., P.O. Box 990, Witkoppen 2068 • *Phone/Fax:* 2711-7012233
• orders@psdprom.co.za • **Distributed in Canada by:** Raincoast • 9050
Shaughnessy St., Vancouver, B.C. V6P 6E5 • *Phone:* (604) 323-7100 •
Fax: (604) 323-2600

Design: Rhett Nacson • *Cover images:* Photo Alto, Facial Moods,
Isabelle Rozenbaum

ISBN 1-4019-0247-2

08   07   06   05   4 3 2 1
1st printing, March 2005

Printed in the United States of America

PASSIONATE
PEOPLE
PRODUCE

REKINDLE YOUR PASSION AND CREATIVITY

Charles Kovess

"This book can show you how to pursue *your* passion. As I read through it, I was constantly thinking 'I could use that,' or 'I could try that.' *Passionate People Produce* is suitable for all ages. There is something of value in each chapter that is relevant to me and to anybody interested in their own personal development."

—Kevin Sheedy,
coach, Essendon Football Club,
Victoria

"If you have anything at all to do with people, be it employer, manager, employee, parent, teacher, mentor or coach, Charles Kovess' book *Passionate People Produce* is essential reading. Its simplicity and wisdom creates a powerful paradigm shift in human relationships that brings out the best in every individual."

—Keith Cummins,
agriculturalist, professional speaker and trainer,
Cohuna, Victoria

"There are some powerful insights in this book, that I am finding to be most useful in both my business life and elsewhere."

—Michael J Sheehan,
head of Global Money Markets & Funding,
National Australia Bank, Melbourne

"This book is valuable for all ages. I have coached for many years, taught for many years, and the insights and ideas are relevant for sport and for business. I am happy to recommend the book to anyone!"

—Steven Raskovy,
Australian Olympian,
Croydon, Victoria

"I was thrilled to read your book after attending one of your seminars. Thank you for coming into my life and reminding me of what it feels like to be passionate. Having read your introduction, I know that I am the one for whom you wrote this book. You raised my passion level, and for that I can't thank you enough."

—Alan G Morgan,
real estate valuer, chartered accountant,
Geelong, Victoria

"This book is truly in alignment with the author's deeply held beliefs. That's what gives it impact."

—Marcia Griffin,
1995 Telstra Businesswoman of the Year,
South Yarra, Victoria

"I have just finished your book. Congratulations on its content. This book is not only for business, but is important for our younger generation of employees who would benefit greatly from acknowledging their inner voice. You now have the means and the platform to project your passion: I hope it will help and encourage children to enlightenment and so change the future."

—Janet Preston,
Vermont, Victoria

"I am truly inspired by the words of wisdom in *Passionate People Produce*."

—Annette Dunlop,
Birkdale, Queensland

"From my own and our organisation's point of view, we have greatly benefitted from Charles Kovess and *Passionate People Produce*. It has been an integral part of our ongoing commitment to development as better people doing something we love."

—Scott Clayton,
Director of Football,
Brisbane Lions Australian Football Club,
Queensland

"Thank you for your inspiration, which I found confirming."

—David Sullivan,
psychologist,
Geelong, Victoria

"I feel compelled to write to you and thank you for your wonderful book. This could not have been read by me at a better time. It was great to see in print things I had felt and believed, but struggled to put into words. You, however, did this brilliantly.

"In February 97, I resigned from a well-paid sales position to pursue my passion by setting up Carenet Family Care Inc., an organisation designed to give practical assistance to sick children and their families. *Passionate People Produce* has confirmed to me that I am doing the right thing, and that my life will continue to be a very exciting, successful and fulfilling adventure for as long as I pursue my passion. I wholeheartedly commend and recommend this book to anyone who does not wake up every morning with a sense of excitement and anticipation. My energy level is through the roof now, and I have never felt so fulfilled."

—Richard Paterson,
co-ordinator, Carenet Family Care, Inc.,
Templestowe, Victoria

To my mother and father, Helen and Zoltan,
to my four wonderful children,
Rebecca, Matthew, Timothy, and Nicholas…
thanks for your love and all of the lessons!

From the Editor:

To our American readers, please note that in some cases we have maintained the Australian-style spelling, grammar, punctuation, and syntax of the original text in order to preserve the editorial intent of the author (who hails from Down Under).

ACKNOWLEDGMENTS

Much of my life has been spent using and writing words in very specific and precise ways, particularly the period from 1969 when I started working during holidays in a legal practice, through to June 1993 when I ceased practising as a lawyer.

Whilst I was well rewarded for my writing efforts, I discovered how difficult the writing process can be; consequently, many years ago I made the decision that I would hate to write a book, and that I would never do so!

So much for resolutions!

Now, almost 18 months after commencing it, the task is done, and I wish to thank the following for their special contributions:

My wife, Jenny, and my children Rebecca, Matthew, Timothy, and Nicholas for their love, for their lessons, and for letting me sit at my computer to write instead of spending time with them.

Joseph Kovess, my brother, who spent many hours in editing and helping to finalize the book's layout, including preparation of the index.

Glenda McNaught, an exceptional lady and English language wordsmith, for her insights and for editorial and grammatical contributions.

Leon Nacson for his encouragement over the last three years.

Marcia Griffin, whose suggestion in 1992 led to many changes in my life.

Yvonne Evans, one of the co-founders of Kovess International Training & Development Pty Ltd (originally 'Kovess Evans Training & Development Pty Ltd') and my business partner for two years, for the gift of many insights, and much learning and wisdom.

Rhett Nacson for his creative design talents.

Sally Moss for her editorial talents.

Geoff Phillips for his friendship and encouragement, particularly during some tough times.

Antony D. Robb for his friendship, encouragement and support.

My fellow 'Full Tilters,' especially Kevin Bolt, for their challenges and support.

My running team members, Ron Preston, Stewart Goodman, Martin Unterwurzacher, Steve James, Graham Gibson, Lisa Nicholson, Michael Bloom, Wayne Noble and Phil Hain, with whom I have trained for 13 years, for their friendship and challenges.

My many teachers and mentors, especially:

Zoltan and Helen Kovess

Father Zoltan Varga S.J.

Stuart Purnell

Matthew J. Walsh

The first edition of this book was published in late 1997. More than seven years later, I can safely say that without the ongoing help, support, encouragement and provocation of many, my dreams would be much further from realization than they now are!

In addition to those I acknowledged in the first edition, most of whom have continued to play important parts in my life, I now acknowledge the following:

Mike Sheehan for his trust and ideas

Sue Wilson and Christopher Bailey for their contribution to my business

Colin Benjamin for his insights and his willingness to share

Pete Crofts for his coaching brilliance

Debbie Tawse for her support as my bureau in New Zealand, and as a friend

Christopher Schulz for his ongoing encouragement

Bob Annells for his support

Bruce Heymanson for his trust and investment

My additional running team members, Luke Goodman, Kip Homewood and Maurie Lazarus, who together with the original team members have played their parts in maintaining my fitness for triathlons for over 18 years.

Dave Wood for his poetic skills and contribution to my business.

My many teachers over the last eight years, who have masqueraded as 'clients'; they are the ones who continually challenged me to refine my ideas, my perspectives, and my beliefs. I wish to particularly acknowledge Andrew Moon, Maurice Pitard, Garry Austin, John Higgins, David Mallard, Rene den Hartog, Chris Chandler, the team at Deakin Prime, Peter Towell, Craig Walton, Geoff Willis, and Catherine Rumberg.

CONTENTS

CHAPTER 8.
HOW TO PROTECT OR ENCOURAGE
PASSION IN YOUR CHILD ·················· 155

CHAPTER 9.
SPECIFIC STRATEGIES FOR YOUR
CHILD AT SCHOOL ···················· 183

INTRODUCTION

I believe that finding one's passion, and then pursuing it, is the key to a life of fulfillment, achievement and learning. I also believe that thousands of years of human experiences clearly demonstrate and, indeed, prove, that passionate people *are* the extraordinary producers.

I believe that passion was what Christ was talking about when he said:

> *What good does it do you when you gain the whole world and lose your soul?*

Religious organizations would suggest that the message in this passage is to avoid the risk of pursuing money in this life because you will miss out on 'heaven' in the next. I suggest that Christ was telling us that pursuing what our soul wants is the key to life, and that if we gain the whole world whilst fulfilling our soul's desire, then we will not lose our souls!

You might find other concepts more comfortable, or less confronting, than that of passion; concepts such as:

- soul
- what you love to do
- what spontaneously arouses you
- what excites you

and so on.

Today, in the Western world at least, there is no shortage of skills. There are plenty of doctors, lawyers, engineers, artists, manufacturers, primary producers. We are urged to look for a gap in the employment market so that we can 'get a job'! This suggests that the key goal of our lives, of our education, is to simply be able to get a job. 'If your work is also your passion, that is wonderful,' say the pragmatists, 'but do not expect such fortune. Life is just not like that!'

The goal of this book is to show that this is not how it is, that making a commitment to finding your passion, and then pursuing it, is a much better way to tackle this educational experience called 'life.' If you desire to produce 'out of the ordinary' results in your life, then passion is the key to that productive process.

I believe that we human beings have been given this gift of passion so that we can know when we are 'on track,' or 'on target': our passion is like a guidepost toward our true purpose, and when we are not passionate, then it is likely that we are not pursuing our unique life's purpose. Discovery by each person of his or her life's purpose is the greatest quest possible.

So what are the hallmarks of a passionate person? How would you describe such a person? For me, passionate people exude energy, power, excitement, drive and commitment. Their eyes sparkle; they are fully alive. They have an impact on others. They are the people who often become our leaders, or become the achievers on this planet. They achieve what they want, and others talk about them and often envy them.

I have asked thousands of people over many years in all of the states of Australia, and other countries, both privately, and publicly in my seminar programs, to indicate what percentage of the working population has impressed them as being 'passionate' about their work. The overwhelming majority say that less than 10 percent of people are visibly pursuing their passion.

This is a modern-day tragedy, and a continuation of it will lead humanity inexorably down the path of misery, scarcity and struggle.

My desire to contribute to changing this prognosis for humanity's future is my motivation for writing this book, much of the content of which arises from training and development programs I have conducted for both individuals and corporations.

If, by reading this book, just one person is inspired to realise what a price is paid in terms of our true humanity when failing to follow our passion, then the book's purpose has been achieved.

— **Charles B. Kovess**
July 1, 1997

***

I am delighted to say that the purpose of this book has already been achieved! Numerous readers have given to me the joy of knowing that this book has made a significant and positive difference to them.

I express my gratitude to them.

Now in 2005, we have entered into a new millennium. We have also experienced extraordinary terrorist attacks on the USA and elsewhere. Has humanity's prognosis of the future been changed since this book was first published?

Many thousands of people over the past nine years have heard me speak of the power and value of passion in their lives, both in keynote presentations and longer workshops and seminars. The word *passion* itself appears in the daily press and the business media with increasing frequency. I am willing to take some credit for this increasing awareness.

This increasing awareness gives me much cause for optimism that our future is becoming more secure. Passion is a source of courage, and I believe courage is the prime capability of true leaders. The future of our planet requires courageous leaders, with a vision that will allow more than just a small minority of humanity to be able to live lives of peace, security, hope, and abundance.

Achievement of such a vision requires long-term, rather than short-term, thinking. It requires behavior that is unconventional. It requires risk-taking. Passion is the source of all of these. I therefore hope that this book plays a part in achieving such a vision. If it does, the future for all of us will be a better one.

— **Charles B. Kovess**
Australia's Passion Provocateur
Spring 2005

CHAPTER 1
What Is Passion?

*'Passion is a source of unlimited energy
from your soul that enables you to
produce extraordinary results!'*

— **Charles Kovess**

*P*assion is not an intellectual thought. It is a feeling, an emotion.

Throughout this book I emphasize the distinction between 'thoughts' and 'feelings.' While both are critically important, it is unfortunate that in today's world thoughts seem to be valued more highly than feelings; that reason, logic and clear thinking, seem to be valued more than feelings, intuition and soul.

Edward de Bono explores why this is so in his wonderful book *Parallel Thinking,* where he highlights the impact that Plato, Socrates, and Aristotle have had on the development of the Western mind.

The 3,000-year-long influence of these thinkers, who believed in the concept of ultimate 'truth,' has militated against our ability today to safely follow intuition, feelings, and passion. I do not need to go into the reasons why this happened, but at a time when survival of the species was in question, a concentration on attending to the bare necessities of survival—food, clothing, and shelter—made some sense. But today, there is an abundance of such necessities and no shortage of raw materials and skills to continue providing them. There is, of course, a serious problem facing distribution of these resources among the world's people, but I see this as being a political problem, not one of scarcity, and beyond the scope of this book, although I do have a vision that an increase of passionate people throughout the world will, indeed, have a positive impact on such political problems.

What does captivate and excite me is the complexity of human behavior, which emanates from our minds, bodies, souls, and emotions combined. We do not exactly know how these human components work together, but slowly, early in the twenty-first century, we appear to be making some progress in our understanding of their interplay. There now seems to be a secular willingness to allow that human beings have a metaphysical dimension—one that cannot be explained by scientific laws of physics and chemistry, and need not have religious connotations.

The spectacular popular success of Dr. Deepak Chopra's book *Ageless Body, Timeless Mind* and James Redfield's *The Celestine Prophecy* is proof on two different platforms of this increasing interest in, and awareness and acceptance of, humanity's great potential.

I believe that this potential is most easily accessed through the experience that we call 'passion.'

Passion can be difficult to find—and many adults fail to find it altogether. In the absence of any encouragement, they give up searching for it, or at least rediscovering it. Who ever heard of grown-ups searching for passion? 'Isn't that something you have as a child, or a young adult, before reality sets in, and you need to feed yourself, and practicality and survival demand that you just get a job, any job!'

Passion similar to 'love.' It is difficult, probably impossible, to define in precise terms, but easy to see and feel when it is present. Let's look at some of its typical elements, symptoms, or signs.

A BURNING DESIRE OR HUNGER

Mahatma Gandhi had a burning desire or hunger to help his fellow human beings. He had a burning desire to spread awareness of two basic principles—truth and non-violence—and his vision was so powerful that these principles were indeed eventually adopted by most people in his country. Gandhi was a passionate man, and his passion enabled him to produce extraordinary results.

Another example of such a burning desire is Australian literary agent Selwa Anthony. While I have not met Selwa Anthony, an article by Antonella Gambotto in **'The Australian Magazine'** of May 3–4, 1997, took my attention. The headline read: 'Agent Selwa Anthony has a cause: popularising the books of Australian writers. Her passion has helped many in publishing, and burned others.'

I was impressed by the following quotes in the article:

> 'When I believe in something,' Anthony insists, 'it's that passion that pushes it to the next stage. If I'm really 100% sold on something, it will get published. I trust my gut instincts.'

'Her passionate convictions, brazen self-confidence, successes and disdain of elitism have won her few followers in the higher literary spheres.'

'Her core belief is that one can be involved in business without "forgetting your heart." She believes the (book publishing) industry is no longer run by those who love books…'

A FEELING OF INSPIRATION

Patanjali, the reputed author (or one of several authors) of two great Hindu classics written in the second century B.C., the *Yoga Sutras* (a categorization of Yogic thought in four volumes) and the *Mahabhasya* (*Great Commentary*), gave a wonderful description of what happens when you are passionate; the quote is useful because it helps us to decide whether or not we are passionate about something. Patanjali wrote:

When you are inspired by some great purpose, some extraordinary project, all your thoughts break their bonds. Your mind transcends limitations, your consciousness expands in every direction, and you find yourself in a new, great and wonderful world. Dormant forces, faculties and talents become alive, and you discover yourself to be a greater person by far than you ever dreamed yourself to be.

A FEELING IN THE PIT OF THE STOMACH

If thinking about a particular issue, task, or activity gives you a 'hit' in your stomach with nerves, tingling, pressure, or palpitations, you could be passionate.

A SENSE OF EXCITEMENT

Like the example in the preceding paragraph, your excitement may arise in your stomach, or any of your five senses. How do you know you are excited? How would you describe it to your best friend? Where is the excitement located? Where in your body do you feel the emotion?

It can be something you see in your mind's eye; it can be something you hear in your head; it can be the incredible lightness of being; it can be a taste or a smell. Each one of us has a unique mix of these sensual experiences when we are excited. Becoming aware of your own unique mix will help you recognize states of true excitement.

A STATE OF AROUSAL

Being aroused is different to being excited. How different is it for you? Sometimes, the passion could be an arousal caused by an injustice, such as unjust treatment of children. That state of arousal is different from an 'excited' state.

A FEELING OF LIMITLESS ENERGY

Passionate people do not easily get tired. Kevin Sheedy, long-standing Australian Football League coach for Essendon, has a phenomenal ability to keep going, to keep talking, to keep watching. His passion feeds him, sustains his body, and overcomes the kind of mental activity that might make a less passionate person feel tired. Kevin is recognized as a man in pursuit of his passion.

Which people around you demonstrate such limitless energy? Would you describe them as passionate? Do you envy their energy, their apparent ability to work harder than most people? Another sports person who demonstrates these characteristics is Brian Goorjian. A profile of Brian Goorjian, coach of a Melbourne basketball team in the National Basketball League, appeared in Melbourne's *Age* newspaper on October 31, 1996, written by Philip Johnson. Brian was born in the United States but came to Australia when he was 23 years old.

The article begins: 'Brian Goorjian has a simple but effective philosophy which he applies to life off the basketball court as well as on it; work hard, do the right thing and follow your passion.'

The article goes on to explore the powerful influences of his father and another Australian basketball coach, Lindsay Gaze, in the power of extreme love for a sport. After examining Brian's career in basketball, the writer concludes with:

One suspects that had Goorjian continued in any of his previous jobs (everything from school teaching to being a nightclub parking lot attendant), he would have done as he was taught and worked hard while doing the right thing. But, thankfully for Australian basketball, Brian Goorjian got to follow his passion.

Brian's achievements as a coach, through following his passion, have been outstanding.

THE FEELING THAT 'I SHOULDN'T BE PAID FOR DOING THIS; I AM HAVING TOO MUCH FUN!'

The way that we earn a living, or work, does not have to be boring, dull, and uninspiring. However, the statistic I quoted earlier—that less than 10 percent of workers in Australia impress their fellow workers as being passionate—can easily cause most people to believe that work, almost by definition, is a struggle and something that can only be enjoyed in exceptional or unusual times.

If you are not passionate about your work, then it is hard to see how it could be fun. What would it be like if work was so much fun that you would do it for nothing? Or, alternatively, if you had $10 million in the bank, would you do the work you are now doing? If the answer is 'yes,' you are clearly passionate.

THE BELIEF THAT NOTHING IS TOO MUCH TROUBLE

A Passion for Excellence is the powerful title of a book by Tom Peters. It also describes in beautiful simplicity the concept of doing or completing a task with a sense that nothing is too much trouble, that the key is to create a result, regardless of the time or effort required.

In my 20 years of practicing law, there were many occasions on which completing the job for my client took precedence over the profit that I could earn. I ignored the cost-benefit analysis: I had a passion for the outcome—and taking that extra step, such as staying up all night to ensure justice and fairness, was not too much!

The rewards for me, in those circumstances, were greater than the fees. The rewards for a job well done, of a grateful client, of seeing a little more fairness, created a sense of well-being that generated and fueled the desire to repeat such moments.

These are the moments when we are fully alive!

A CLARITY OF VISION

According to practitioners of Neurolinguistic Programming, most people can 'see' a picture in their mind's eye when they are asked to imagine something. Can you 'see' what business or enterprise you are trying to create for the future? Can you see how it will operate?

The quality of the picture in your mind's eye will demonstrate to you the power of your passion. Passionate people have a spectacularly clear picture of what they want to create, of how the world will be when they have achieved their passion.

Great athletes have such an ability to 'see' into the future. The power and clarity of this vision, produced by passion, is the power that energizes champions to 'go the extra mile,' to make the extra effort. They can see the results of their efforts, years into the future.

When I competed in surf-lifesaving competitions with the Lorne Surf Life Saving Club, Don Heathcote was my coach. He had a passion for the Rescue and Resuscitation Competition, and could see what it would mean for him, for the Lorne Club and for Victorian surf lifesaving generally if he could coach the winning Australian Champion R&R Team. Back in the 1960s, no Victorian team had ever won this competition. Yet it was always considered to be the event that determined the 'Premiership of Australia.' He struggled for years, and inspired many young swimmers, before he achieved his vision in March of 1973.

Many people had told him that he was mad, he was impractical, and that there was no chance of success.

Don did not believe any of them, and it was the power of his vision that enabled him to inspire his team to ignore the knockers. Young lifesavers, who had not decided what area they'd like to compete in, would be wooed by Don, who would tell them what it would be like to 'climb the mountain,' what it would be like to be Australian champions.

A SENSE OF CARING DEEPLY

What do you care about? Who do you care about? This is a slightly different experience from the feeling that nothing is too much trouble, but when you care, you have greater energy, a greater ability to create, a greater ability to produce. Caring comes from a part of us that is more than body or mind: it is a soul connection, or a heart-to-heart connection. A man who cares appears to be Steve Jobs, the creator of Apple Computer. A profile of Steve Jobs appeared in Melbourne's *Age* newspaper on May 27, 1997, written by Garry Barker. The headline read:

'Steve Jobs: The Passion Burns Anew'

Relevant parts of the article follow:

If you listen, as I did … to Steve Jobs talking about Apple… it's hard not to fall into open-mouthed awe. The man is a spell binder…Jobs has a passion that sets him apart; puts him on a plane different from that on which Microsoft's Bill Gates makes his billions. Jobs has juice where Gates has money.

He has matured and mellowed since the days when Apple sat on top of the world, but he still radiates enormous enthusiasm—for all his faults, Jobs is one of those who made Macintosh what it is; gave it its soul.

Jobs is quoted in the article as saying:

'Every good product I have ever seen in this industry came about because people cared deeply about making something wonderful that they and their friends wanted.'

OTHER DEFINITIONS OF *Passion*

The *Oxford Companion to Philosophy* (edited by Ted Honderich, Oxford University Press, 1995) says passion is 'any strong desire or feeling.' It goes on:

The term *passion* has a long and convoluted history, however, both in and out of philosophy. Although passion is often identified with emotion, the two are not the same. Descartes, for example, treats emotions as the subspecies of particularly disturbing passions. The ancients often treated passion as a kind of madness, and the Stoics diagnosed the passions as profound and often fatal misunderstandings. Modern philosophers have treated them as 'confused perceptions' and 'distorted judgments.' The word *passion* originally meant suffering, as in the 'passion of Christ,' and the passions themselves have suffered in philosophy from their unflattering juxtaposition with reason. Whereas reason is what is most human (even divine) about us, the passions make us their victims, 'sweep us away.' The Greek

Aesop summed up the view of most philosophers, which is that reason must be the master of the passions. It was against this long-standing advice that David Hume made his shocking announcement that 'reason is and ought to be the slave of passions.' Ever since ancient times, of course, there have been certain 'romantics' and many others who would give the passions their due. 'Nothing great has ever been done without passion,' insisted Hegel, but even Kant said it before him. What is necessary is for the distinction itself to be brought into question. Nietzsche: 'as if every passion did not contain its own quantum of reason.'

Kahlil Gibran in *The Prophet*, explored this dichotomy between passion and reason. He wrote:

> Your soul is oftentimes a battlefield, upon which your reason and your judgment wage war against your passion and your appetite…
>
> Your reason and your passion are the rudder and the sails of your seafaring soul.
>
> If either your sails or your rudder be broken, you can but toss and drift, or else be held at a standstill in mid-seas.
>
> For reason, ruling alone, is a force confining; and passion, unattended, is a flame that burns to its own destruction.

Gibran then went on to acknowledge the importance and relevance of both. He equated them to two guests in our houses: and asked us not to favor either.

My belief, and the point I want to make here, is that our Western world values reason much more highly than passion.

That is the tragedy. If the two are treated as Gibran would have had us do, then great changes are possible. A whole new capacity in us can be opened up.

Ralph Waldo Emerson gave this advice in *Self Reliance*:

'Nothing is at last sacred but the integrity of your own mind.'

That is another reason why passion is important, because following your passion increases the chances of being in integrity with yourself. Emerson's thought was coupled with his assurance that

'in yourself is the law of all nature…in yourself slumbers the whole of reason' .

My view of integrity is that it means being true to myself. It is quite different to honesty, although in my experience many equate, or even confuse, the two. How do I know that I am being true to myself? Unless I know myself, I will never know! And getting to know myself is the great quest of life. Without self-knowledge, we cannot be wise, we cannot have wisdom.

On the subject of integrity, the *Oxford Companion to Philosophy* has this to say:

The quality of a person who can be counted upon to give precedence to moral considerations, even when there is strong inducement to let self-interest or some clamant desire override them, or where the betrayal of moral principle might pass undetected. To have integrity is to have unconditional and steady commitment to moral values and obligations. For such a person, the fundamental question whether to conduct life on the plane of self-concern or of moral seriousness has been decisively resolved, though particular life situations will doubtless continue to put that commitment to strenuous test. This moral commitment becomes a crucial component in his or her sense of identity as a person: it confers a unity (integration) of character, and even a simplicity upon the man or woman of integrity. What integrity cannot guarantee is the soundness of the value judgments themselves, which form the core of that person's commitment.

The value judgments we make, the morals we adopt, all require a knowledge of self, because these judgments and morals, unless slavishly adopted from our parents or other people of influence, are how each one of us 'sees' the world through the filter of our own mind. And our minds create our reality, based upon what lies within. How much is true in that 'swamp' of the unconscious? That is what the search for self-knowledge answers, and it is often a difficult search, with few signposts.

Integrity, according to the *Shorter Oxford English Dictionary*, is:

> The condition of having no part or element wanting; unbroken state; material wholeness, completeness, entirety. Unimpaired or uncorrupted state; original perfect condition; soundness. Soundness of moral principle; the character of uncorrupted virtue; uprightness, honesty, sincerity.

How do emotions and passion sit together? Indeed, what are emotions? This book is not going to traverse this field, save to say that the question is complicated and in dispute. However, the *Oxford Companion to Philosophy*, in its discussion on 'emotion and feeling,' makes a useful contribution to the 'passion vs reason' debate:

> If there are necessary connections between knowledge and emotion, emotions can be seen as rational ways of perceiving and interacting with the world, rather than random, self-enclosed psychic or physical sensations. The assumption initiated by Plato that emotions distort or obscure the true way of seeing the world, because they conflict with reason, can be replaced by the view that they complement reason and open up the realms of moral, aesthetic, and religious values.

The *Companion* goes on to say: 'Psychoanalytic theories make emotion a matter of reacting to something in our unconscious, not something in reality.' The *Shorter Oxford English Dictionary* gives this definition of *passion*:

> An affection of the mind. Any vehement, commanding, or overpowering emotions; in psychology or art, any mode in which the mind is affected or acted upon, as ambition, avarice, desire, hope, fear, love, hatred, joy, grief, anger, revenge. A fit or mood of excited feeling; an outburst of feeling. A sexual desire or impulse. An overmastering zeal or enthusiasm for some object. An aim or object pursued with zeal.

I am now writing this section shortly after Christmas 1996. For Christmas, my then-wife, Jenny, gave to me the book *Conversations with God...an uncommon dialogue*, by Neale Donald Walsch. It is an extraordinary book, and Jenny found it when she walked into the bookstore, asking her spirit to direct her to the 'right' book for me. Within ten seconds she found it.

Walsch claims to have faithfully recorded his conversations with God. The positive and uplifting experiences and feelings that I had while reading the book are supportive of Walsch's claim.

As quoted by Walsch, God talks of passion in this way:

Therefore, judge not that about which you feel passionate. Simply notice it, then see if it serves you, given who and what you wish to be.

Remember, you are constantly in the act of creating yourself. You are in every moment deciding who and what you are. You decide this largely through the choices you make regarding who and what you feel passionate about. Often a person on what you call a spiritual path looks like he has renounced all earthly passion, all human desire. What he has done is understand it, see the illusion, and step aside from the passions that do not serve him—all the while loving the illusion for what it has brought to him: the chance to be wholly free.

Passion is the love of turning being into action. It fuels the engine of creation. It changes concepts to experience. Passion is the fire that drives us to express who we really are. Never deny passion, for that is to deny Who You Are and Who You Truly Want to Be.

The renunciate never denies passion—the renunciate simply denies attachment to results. Passion is a love of doing. Doing is being, experienced. Yet what is often created as part of doing? Expectation.

To live your life without expectation—without the need for specific results—that is freedom. That is Godliness. That is how I live.

I added the above thoughts to Chapter 1 while halfway through this book, because they reinforced my reasons for writing the book and helped me to fight the urge not to write it. When I had not written for weeks at a time and analyzed what was getting in the way of writing, I realized that I was doubting that what I had to say was worth saying.

I lost those doubts, and I was delighted to do so!

MY DEFINITION OF *Passion*

Some talented writers have attempted to define *passion*, and I had some hesitation in following their lead. However, a review of both my own life, and the lives of those who have had the greatest impact upon me, have enabled me to develop a clear set of words which convey my understanding of the subject. For me,

> *passion is a source of unlimited energy from the soul (or 'spirit' of 'heart' that enables a person to produce extraordinary results.*

The two key words are *energy* and *soul*, and the reasons for choosing these words will be apparent from the preceding thoughts in this Chapter 1.

KEY POINTS FOR CHAPTER 1

- Review the subheads in this chapter.
- It's time to change the emphasis we give to reason over feelings and emotions.
- If you want to be outstanding, you must be passionate.
- Passion is a different and unique experience for each person.
- When you follow your passion, you unleash enormous reserves of energy and courage: That's why passionate people produce!

CHAPTER 2
How to Find Your Passion

CHAPTER 2
How to Find Your Passion

'Without passion, man is a mere latent force and possibility, like the flint which awaits the shock of the iron before it can give forth its spark.'

— Henri-Frederic Amiel

I believe that every human being is designed to be passionate, that passion lies within all of us. However, passion is like a flame in our hearts: it slowly and inexorably dies if it is not fueled. Ignoring passion is like failing to put more wood on the fire.

Fortunately, the flame never dies entirely, because we have our memories, and those memories ensure that the flame can always be rekindled. It can be rekindled when we start to pursue our passion.

However, to start discovering and pursuing our passion we need to have a clear understanding of possible outcomes. What will the specific benefits be for you if you find your passion? What will that give you? How will you feel? If you are in doubt about what you might feel, reread Patanjali's quote in Chapter 1.

The more clearly you can articulate the answers to these questions, the greater the likelihood that you will take the steps needed to find your passion. Changing our behavior is usually very difficult, and change takes place only if there is a strong enough reason or motivator. I urge you to be aware of this fundamental principle of our human nature.

Passion and the Threat to Comfort

What could prevent you from discovering your passion? One block to discovering passion can be our need for comfort. How comfortable are you? Is your existing comfort, albeit not an inspiring one, stopping you from looking for your passion? Do you have enough pain to motivate you to get out of your comfort zone?

Kahlil Gibran, in *The Prophet*, deals with this challenge beautifully. The prophet is talking of houses:

What have you in these houses? And what is it you guard with fastened doors?

Have you peace?...Have you remembrances?

...Have you beauty, that leads the heart from things fashioned of wood and stone to the holy mountain?

Tell me, have you these in your houses?

Or have you only comfort, and the lust for comfort, that stealthy thing that enters the house a guest, and then becomes a host, and then a master?

Ay, and it becomes a tamer, and with hook and scourge makes puppets of your larger desires.

Though its hands are silken, its heart is of iron.

It lulls you to sleep only to stand by your bed and jeer at the dignity of the flesh.

It makes mock of your sound senses, and lays them in thistledown like fragile vessels.

He then comes to this telling conclusion: 'Verily the lust for comfort murders the passion of the soul, and then walks grinning in the funeral.'

THE NEED TO TAKE A RISK: JUDGE PETER GEBHARDT

A man who demonstrated his willingness to forsake comfort, and to take a risk in pursuing a totally new career, is Judge Peter Gebhardt. A profile of Judge Gebhardt appeared in Melbourne's *Age* newspaper on November 1, 1996, written by Michael Gawenda.

Judge Gebhardt is extraordinary for a number of reasons. First, he is a published poet and a judge. Second, he was a teacher for 25 years before beginning his practice as a lawyer, despite having gained his legal qualifications shortly after leaving school. Third, he left the teaching profession and took a significant risk at the age of 50 in changing his career. The article states:

> Before he opted for the law, Peter Gebhardt had devoted his working life to teaching, starting out as a teacher at Geelong Grammar in 1959 and finishing his teaching career with a decade as headmaster of Geelong College from 1975 until 1985.
>
> At that point, Peter Gebhardt decided it was time to re-evaluate his life, to look at what he wanted to do with the second half of a life…that had seen him achieve everything he wanted to achieve in teaching.

He is quoted as saying:

> I had done a law degree at Melbourne University before I went into teaching, but I had not wanted to

become a lawyer…I didn't even do articles. Then, when I knew my time in teaching was ending, I thought I'd give the law a go. I did my articles at 50, and started out as a barrister, on my own, at 51. It was tough, but people were kind to me.

SPECIFIC STRATEGIES

People have also told me they cannot remember having felt any passion in the past. So what can be done in these circumstances? What are some specific strategies that you could use to find your passion?

We can start by answering some questions— questions such as:

- What do you love doing?
- What would you do if you had $10 million in the bank?
- What do you hate in the world?
- What makes you angry?
- Which part of your present work is the most enjoyable?
- Which part of your present work comes most easily to you?
- Which part of your past work came most easily to you?
- What is the most upsetting part of your present work?

Let's look at how we might answer each of these.

WHAT DO YOU LOVE DOING?

There must be something you love doing! Each aspect of

your life that you love is a clue to your passion, to your soul. You may think there is nothing, but if this is so, simply make the decision to become aware of what you love in your life.

What you love may be as seemingly innocuous as going to restaurants with friends, or going to the football.

Start a 'Passion Diary.' In the diary list all of the things you love doing. Now ask yourself what it is about these experiences that you find pleasurable.

If your passion is going to restaurants with friends, is it the friendships that you are cultivating? Is it the fact that you are having your meal prepared for you? Is it the energy being generated in the restaurant by people who are feeling good, particularly if this contrasts with your colleagues at work, who may be feeling the opposite? List the pleasurable aspects in your Passion Diary.

One afternoon some years ago, I was having a cup of tea with the wife of one of my relatives. I asked her what her husband loved doing. Her husband is very skilled at carpentry, but her response was that he loved having sex! This was no real surprise to me, particularly because I am the same. I have often wondered about my sex drive, and I have come to the conclusion that it is something to do with being Hungarian, European, Latin, and emotional.

Anyway, this particular couple are not wealthy, and I suggested that her husband could follow his passion by becoming a professional stud! The wife, to her credit, did not fall off her chair. I explained that I knew a number of older ladies who were having great difficulty meeting men to their liking with whom they could express themselves sexually so that someone like her husband could play a role.

Most of these ladies were wealthy, and would be willing to pay for reliable male 'companionship.' I knew her husband would have been physically capable of satisfying these ladies and the financial rewards would have been large.

There would have been a risk to my relative in pursuing this course: the risk of others 'judging' his activities, judging his morals, and perhaps rejecting him and his wife as a consequence. At law, nothing was stopping him. It was only a matter of courage to follow his own needs and desires and passion, and not to need the approval of others.

This example demonstrates that we often have to pay a price for doing what we love to do. Oh, that it were not so, but our rewards as human beings seem to follow this pattern: the greater the price we are willing to pay, the greater is the reward. The price can be loss of friendships, loss of spouse, loss of money, loss of security, and so on, but the benefits can be correspondingly significant: that is what this book is about, to explore the links between following your passion, thereby producing the extraordinary results of which you are capable, and understanding the risks that you may have to take, and the pain that you may have to bear, through the process.

If you cannot remember what you loved in the past, just keep on reading! The ideas that are explored in this book will help jog your memory, or at the very least will demonstrate ways to recall those special events.

WHAT WOULD YOU DO IF YOU HAD $10 MILLION IN THE BANK?

I have found this to be a most revealing question. Survival is clearly a powerful instinct, and much of what we human beings do is geared to earning money so that we can survive. And yet, the economic theory that is slavishly adopted by most people—the theory, declared by Thomas Malthus in the early nineteenth century, that survival for humans on this planet was destined to become harder and harder because our population was increasing at an exponential rate but our resources were increasing only on a 'straight line' basis—is flawed.

Malthus pronounced his theory after he had considered the results of a worldwide inventory of the planet's resources. It is wrong because the theory ignores mankind's extraordinary capacity for discovering new and better ways to do everything—our capacity for doing more with less. (For a detailed exposition of this notion, I recommend Buckminster Fuller's *Critical Path*.)

Malthus's theory has caused much grief and heartache, because it has created a 'dog-eat-dog' culture, a culture of scarcity, a culture of 'I win, you lose' since both of us cannot be winners. Survival, we are taught, is tough, so we need to pursue money-making activities that are the most likely to generate money, rather than pursuing our passion.

It can be difficult breaking free of this falsity. Our psychological makeup is designed to ensure our survival, so if we believe what we are taught, we are trapped. One way of breaking free, to explore what might be possible, is to imagine that you have no financial pressures, that you have $10 million in the bank.

What would you do in these circumstances? How would your life be? What would interest you? What would excite you? Who would you help? Listen carefully to your intuitive answers to each of these questions: they are valuable clues which will become signposts as you continue to read this book. The accumulation of these signposts will determine the road you follow.

Write your answers in your Passion Diary.

WHAT DO YOU HATE IN THE WORLD?

What you hate can be a valuable clue to your passion. Do you hate injustice? Do you hate the abuse of children? Do you hate poverty? Do you hate the harm being done to our planet's environment in the name of economic progress, in the name of survival? Do you hate capitalism?

Or, like me, do you hate the fact that our Western system of thought and behavior discourages us, or prevents us, from pursuing our passion? (In my case, that hate is partly responsible for the fact that I ceased to practice law after twenty years and established a new business in the field of training and development. It is that hate that has partly inspired me to write this book.)

Hate is a very powerful feeling, and is a valuable clue to our true essence. Perhaps your purpose will be fulfilled if you take steps to rid the world of the things that you hate.

WHAT MAKES YOU ANGRY?

Anger is different from hate. The differences are very subtle, and there is no guidebook available to tell us which is which. My only advice is to become increasingly aware of exactly what it is that you are feeling at a particular time. Nevertheless, at this point in time, it is not necessary to explore this distinction. If you do not hate something but you are angry about it, then that awareness is the useful clue.

So what makes you angry? It could be politicians who do not tell the truth. It could be the distribution of food on our planet, which leads to massive overproduction in some places and abject starvation in others. It could be victimization of children in the schoolyard by bullies, or victimization of students by teachers.

On this latter point, I have experienced a few teachers whose strategy for 'encouraging' learning is to use humiliation. They make fun of those students who do not know the correct answer, with the misguided view that the pain of humiliation will become a powerful incentive to learn.

For some students, this strategy works. In my case, for example, it certainly worked: while I was a successful student, I also wanted to avoid the humiliation, and on the few occasions when I was humiliated, or 'put down,' I was spurred on by the vow 'he's not going to do that to me again!' However, for many others, humiliation destroys self-esteem, which leads inexorably to a lifelong fear of learning.

My former wife, Jenny, while attending a highly renowned private girls school at the tender age of nine, was made by her mathematics teacher to stand in front of the class to answer questions. When the correct answer was not forthcoming, the teacher encouraged the rest of the class to laugh at Jenny!

Fortunately, the teacher was eventually removed from teaching duties after complaints from parents of other children, but Jenny's experiences have continued to affect her day-to-day life. Thirty-one years later, Jenny still has a terror of both speaking in public and learning new skills in the field of mathematics. She is successfully addressing both issues, and the awareness of the source of the fear has been helpful.

Listen carefully to your feelings, and find out what makes you angry. Write it all down. Write a letter to your best friend and express your anger, rather than bottling it up. The process of expressing your anger in words will play a part in raising your awareness of your feelings. That awareness could lead you to your passion!

If you were the victim in the example described above, you could become a passionate promoter of teaching strategies that rule out the use of humiliation and victimization. Your anger at your own treatment could become the fuel that drives you, the fuel that drives your passion. And the pursuit of your passion would become easy because you know, from your own experience, how painful and wasteful it is to destroy a child's self-esteem.

WHICH PART OF YOUR PRESENT WORK IS THE MOST ENJOYABLE?

I said in the introduction to this book that not many people are passionate about their work. That is both my own experience, and the anecdotal evidence that I have gathered over the years from attendees at my training programs.

If you are not passionate about your work, start to become aware of the parts of your work that are the most enjoyable for you. In your Passion Diary, make a list of exactly what it is that you do, and add to the list each day.

Begin to make conscious written evaluations of each favorite task—for example, 'Gee, I like doing this...,' or 'I wish I could do more of this...,' and so on.

One of the challenges in this process may be that the new awareness for you can be a blow to your ego! This can come from the realization that the part of work that is most enjoyable is something that many people, even you, would not hold in high regard. The challenge is to acknowledge this aspect and yet have the courage to start doing more of this part that you enjoy.

When I was practicing as a solicitor, while I was always passionate about the work in its totality, there were some aspects of the work that were more appealing to me than others. I loved it when a new client would hear about me and contact me: not only was this was a real boost to my ego, but meeting new people and hearing the broad outline of a new problem were both very exciting.

However, a few weeks into the problem, when there is some hard work to be done, like researching a particularly esoteric point of law, the excitement level would drop somewhat. This part was harder for me because it did not have the excitement of the first meeting and the building of a new relationship.

By doing more of the parts that I enjoyed the most, and sharing that with my firm, I could have been appointed as a 'rainmaker'—the person who is responsible for marketing the firm and bringing in the new clients. However, playing such a role would certainly not have expanded my technical legal knowledge, and would not have enhanced my reputation as a skilled lawyer—and both of these impediments would have been a blow to my ego. Why? Because they would have affected how other people thought of me. Blows to the ego usually come from what other people may think of us. Would it not be liberating to not care what anybody thought of you?

WORRIED ABOUT WHAT OTHERS THINK?

Here is a saying that I have found very challenging, and one that has become a personal goal:

'What you think of me is none of my business!'

Truly living by this declaration would free me from ongoing concerns about other people's thoughts and feelings and let me get on with my life. It would enable me to decide freely what is good for me and what is not good for me. I would make my decisions on that basis, and not on the basis of someone else's reality—or at least what I *believe* is their reality.

How do I know I am right? Consider how *difficult* it is to figure out what is going on inside you, and what makes you passionate; isn't it *impossible* to figure out what is going on inside another person?

What is it that drives us to avoid doing anything that others might not approve of? Why do we do things to please others, when these things do not please ourselves? Perhaps the best answer is our fear of rejection, which arises from our desire or need to be loved. Most of us want to be wanted, and we will do almost anything to satisfy that need. The need arises because of our very early experiences in life: we learned, as babies, that if we were rejected by our parents, or were not wanted by them, then our very survival was at stake. The scenario went like this:

If my mother rejects me, she won't come to me when I cry.
If my mother won't come to me when I cry, I'll be hungry.
If I remain hungry for too long, I'll die!

These experiences, learned in an emotional state, become powerful forces in our subconscious minds. I encourage you to become consciously aware of the power that these experiences have created for you, and how they influence your day-to-day decision making. It is only through awareness that we can start to do something about the causes of our present behavior.

'Reality' is another factor in this process. I used to think that there was an objective reality that was the same for everyone. I no longer believe this. I now believe that each one of us creates our own reality: that each one of us has a unique reality, based upon our unique experiences of life. One of my 'realities' used to be that most people see and experience the world as I do, but I now realize how incorrect this was. (Wayne Dyer's book *Your Sacred Self* is one of many recently published books which contains a detailed discussion of this 'reality' question.)

Accordingly, how would we know that other people would think more or less of us if we did what we enjoy doing? How do we know whether someone we love will disapprove of us for pursuing the part of our work that gives us pleasure? How much of this are we guessing, or predicting, based on our unique reality?

Are you stopping yourself from doing more of what you enjoy at work because of some of the above issues? If you become aware that you are, this can be a powerful force for you, to encourage you to pursue your own enjoyment rather than creating enjoyment for others at your cost. By giving yourself permission to pursue your enjoyment, there will be a flow-through effect through to everything you do, and this will give you an ever-increasing awareness that will help you to realize your passion.

I recently had a 'BFO' moment: a 'Blinding Flash of the Obvious.' I was presenting to a group of executives from Optus Communications, one of Australia's major telecommunication companies. On the flipchart I was using, I'd drawn a heart, and then written the word *courage* over the heart. The blinding flash came when I remembered the derivation of the word *courage* It has the same Latin origin as the French word *coeur*: 'cor,' meaning 'heart.' In fact, we exhibit courage when we follow our heart, and the corollary seems to link beautifully: that to follow our hearts often requires great courage!

WHICH PART OF YOUR PRESENT WORK IS THE EASIEST FOR YOU?

Sometimes we can fall into the trap of doing simply what we are good at, even though it does not fulfill us. Many people who are not passionate about their work are still quite competent at that work. The part of your job that is easiest for you can contain the link to finding your passion.

What is this part? Why is it so easy? What is happening inside you when you are doing it? What feelings is it generating in you? The answers to these questions are very valuable: do not discount them.

Remember that something that is easy for you does not *make* it easy per se! Remember your unique reality. If it is easy, you may get a sense of flowing with the work, because it is in alignment with your spirit or your soul. You may get a sense of peace, rather than struggle. Perhaps, because of your own experiences, you have never allowed yourself to appreciate fully the parts of your work, or indeed your life, that come easily to you because you were taught, and you therefore learned, that anything that is worth doing must be a struggle.

WHICH PART OF YOUR PAST WORK CAME MOST EASILY TO YOU?

Look back over your life. Make a list of all of the different types of work that you have been engaged in. Include on the list all of your work as a child. What was easy for you? What has been your attitude to the work that came easily to you? Did you subconsciously discount its value?

When I was 11 years of age, I was working for a news agent, Jack Murphy. I'd been delivering papers early in the mornings, six days a week, for a year, when he asked me whether I wanted to earn more money. He offered me the 'collect.' This was the job of 'collecting' the monies owed to the news agency by its customers to whom papers were delivered. There were four rounds, to be done on Saturday mornings, so that each customer was visited once each month. I accepted.

I got on to my bicycle at 9 A.M. every Saturday and started knocking on doors to collect the money. I found it enjoyable and easy. Meeting the customers, whom I never saw otherwise, was fun. I was not afraid of asking them for money. Being told that they could not pay did not cause me any anguish, even though I was paid on my results (my pay was a percentage of what I actually collected). I knew or believed that if they did not pay me this week, I'd get the money in four weeks' time.

This job was a valuable experience for me, and taught me many lessons. It taught me that doing a job that I found easy could still be fun and profitable. It taught me how to ask for money. As I saw it, the money was owing and there was absolutely no shame or anything to fear in asking for it.

Interestingly, as I grew older, I forgot some of these valuable lessons, and sometimes found it difficult to collect monies owed by my clients when I was practicing as a solicitor. I think I developed a greater fear of rejection as I got older, a fear that, if I upset clients by asking them to pay me, then they may leave me for another solicitor. In hindsight, it is embarrassing to confess this, and I know I allowed it to happen because I was not consciously aware of the source of my fear.

There was perhaps another fear: that my legal work wasn't good enough to demand that the clients pay me. When I was delivering newspapers, I knew that my deliveries were excellent, and that there was no possible cause for complaint by the customers. The practice of law is somewhat more subjective, and my client's reality may have been different to my own.

There was a huge, unanticipated benefit in my agreeing to do the 'collect': I met an extraordinary customer, Stuart Purnell, a solicitor. When I was 11, he was 53, and had been married for almost 20 years. They had no children.

For some reason unknown to me, Stuart took an interest in this little boy who arrived on his doorstep once a month, and I found myself in his home having coffee, discussing jazz, Latin, the law and Shakespeare. These discussions took place while I was supposed to be on the job, so in the end I left Stuart's house until last, because I knew I couldn't 'get away' from him quickly (not that I wanted to, it was just that I had my work to do).

Stuart contributed to my education, and to my life. I had always wanted to be a lawyer, but my father had told me it was very difficult to get a job, particularly as the son of a Hungarian immigrant. That was my father's reality, which in hindsight was incorrect, but I now know he picked up this reality from his fellow Hungarians in Melbourne.

Through meeting Stuart, and becoming his and his wife Evelyn's surrogate son, I lost any fears about my ability to get a job in the law.

Stuart was an extraordinary man, who made an amazing contribution to my life. He was a Greek and Roman historian, spoke fluent Latin, and was learned in Shakespeare and many other aspects of English literature. He loved music, traditional jazz in particular, and the law. His legal practice was a small one, with one secretary, a part time bookkeeper, Evelyn, as his law clerk, and himself. He carried on his practice not for the purpose of making a living, but to make a contribution to the welfare of his clients, and had a wonderful life. His clients loved him, and paid him willingly and happily.

I have no doubt that, if I had not agreed to do the 'collect,' I would have adopted my father's reality and accepted that it was impractical for me to do what I wanted to do, which was to be a lawyer.

Why did I want to be a lawyer? Because ever since I can remember, as a young child, friends of my parents told me that I should be a lawyer. They had noticed that I could, and would, argue anything that would serve my interests. I would argue that black was white, that I was right when in fact I was wrong, that I did not break the window even though I was the only child who could possibly have broken it! And the fact is that I argued in this way because it was easy for me! Because it was easy, adults made suggestions to me, which created in me, or revealed to me, a passion to practice law!

For you, too, what was easy for you in the past could be the critical clue for chasing your passion, for identifying it, and for giving you the permission to pursue it.

What Is the Most Upsetting Part of Your Present Work?

As with your hates and your 'angers,' becoming consciously aware of the most upsetting parts of your work will give you valuable clues to your soul, to your spirit, to your passion.

Here are some real examples of upsetting aspects of work, many of which have been raised in my seminars:

- We get no encouragement from our bosses.
- We get no recognition when we do a good job.
- We get no recognition when we put in a special effort.
- We send bills to our customers even though we have not done a good job.

- Relationships between co-workers are strained and stressful.
- Our bosses treat us like second-class citizens.
- Our bosses think that we are unable to think.
- We are sometimes forced to tell lies to customers.
- We are 'put down' in front of others for making mistakes.

I do not believe that we can be passionate about our work in circumstances such as the above. Our passion can be squashed if it is not nurtured, and each one of us has unique needs for that nurturing, just as plants need different fertilizers, different positions in the garden, and different treatment.

Let's go through a few of the above examples, and see what clues to passion can be found. Remember that we are trying to determine what *most* upsets us. Whilst we can have many minor upsets, it is the major upsets that will give us the best clues to our spirit.

'WE GET NO ENCOURAGEMENT FROM OUR BOSSES'

For most of the twentieth century, the attitude of too many leaders and managers in business has been that the weekly paycheck is the only encouragement needed by employees. This attitude is understandable, particularly in light of the great depression in the 1930s, as well as the two world wars. In many cases, employees were so grateful to have a job that the expectation of encouragement or recognition did not consciously arise. I have heard older employees express the view that those who need encouragement are ungrateful, or childish or that they have something wrong with them!

Times have changed—and they will continue to change, at an ever-increasing pace. Pressures arise from this changeability which did not occur in the past. Greater courage is needed today than previously. Successful businesses need employees who are willing to take risks at testing the boundaries of what is, or is not, possible.

If your organization gives little encouragement or recognition, this may indicate a significant misunderstanding of what is needed to thrive in business today. It may indicate a lack of care for employees. It may indicate a middle-level manager who is not interested in, or does not understand, people. The most upsetting part for you may be that you can see the waste that is occurring as a consequence.

Additionally, you may become aware that, if encouragement was given, then your level of passion would rise dramatically and your contribution to the organization would be much improved. Such an awareness may be the only catalyst you need to begin a reevaluation process within your organization!

In Australia and the United States, surveys of employees and their employers have been conducted to try to ascertain the factors that motivate employees and those that employers *think* motivate employees.

Overwhelmingly, employers considered that most employees are motivated by money. And yet, the consistent response by many thousands of employees put salary in fourth or fifth position, well behind appreciation for a good job, ability to grow and learn, and quality relationships within the workplace, as their 'drivers' or 'motivators'!

'WE SEND BILLS TO OUR CUSTOMERS EVEN THOUGH WE HAVE NOT DONE A GOOD JOB'

This issue highlights a conflict between two values—namely, honesty and wealth.

One of the purposes of a business is to make a profit. Today, in our technological age, many businesses are driven by statistics and time sheets. The pressure is put on employees for performance at a particular level.

Sometimes, jobs are 'stuffed up.' Sometimes, much more time is spent on a task than was necessary. However, it can be easy for the professional service provider, for example, to hide the error or failure. The computer generates the account, and the client is fooled into paying the account, with or without complaint about the amount. The rendering of the account in these circumstances is the wealth value taking priority over the honesty value.

If your 'values hierarchy' or 'scale of values' (more of this a little later) puts honesty ahead of wealth, then the above behavior will have a negative effect on you: it will upset you. An awareness of this mismatch between your own values and those of your organization could cause you to change the situation, or to explore your own values in greater detail. That exploration of values could lead you down a path to your passion.

'RELATIONSHIPS BETWEEN CO-WORKERS ARE STRAINED AND STRESSFUL'

If relationships with other people in the workplace are important to you, and if those relationships are unsatisfying, the passion and pleasure of work can disappear. Things are made even worse when the organization you work in seems unconcerned by strains and stresses in the relationships between its staff.

Recently, I was helping to implement some human resources strategies at a leading menswear wholesaler and retailer (let's call it H Corporation), a company that cared enough about such issues to hire a consultant

The company's receptionist, Nancy, had previously told me that the seven months she'd spent working with H Corporation were among the best in her working career. She enjoyed the people, the work, and the culture, where encouragement and recognition of employees was a high value. The managing director of the company was clear in his mind that relationships with people had a higher value for him than making money. This philosophy generally carried through to the rest of the company's 35 employees.

However, Nancy told me that, in the preceding two weeks, she had been having a much less enjoyable time, due solely to the fact that she believed Nina, the book-keeper, did not like her! And this had arisen because Nina was being a little cool toward her, after being much warmer in the preceding months.

Just imagine this: Nancy's whole attitude to the company and her level of pleasure had changed significantly because of her belief that one person was having a problem with her, whatever that problem may have been. It became my job to find out, and I told Nancy that I would do so.

Unbeknownst to Nancy, some days previously I'd had a long interview with Nina in which I explored Nina's experience at H Corporation, and the things that she considered could be improved. This was a process that I also undertook with other key employees, on a one-on-one basis, to get a true feel of what was really going on.

The questions I'd asked each employee were as follows:

- What upsets you while working at H Corporation?
- Which agreements have not been kept?
- What are the best things about working at H Corporation?
- What are the worst things about working at H Corporation?
- Which improvements would you suggest?
- Are you getting enough feedback on your job?
- What training have you done to date?
- Which skills do you need to develop?
- Which skills do you want to develop?
- Which incentives do you presently get?
- Which incentives do you want in the future?
- What would be the specific benefits of improved teamwork?
- What would that give you?
- What do you think H Corporation can achieve or grow to in the future?
- Do you think there are negative attitudes at present?
- Is there a 'passing the buck' syndrome?
- How can we improve communications throughout the company?
- What specific information has not been passed on to you in the past?

When I discussed these issues with Nina, she told me that Nancy was not pulling her weight, that she was nowhere near as good as Moira, the former receptionist whom she'd replaced a few months earlier. She was upset that Nancy had not put Nina's husband through to her when he'd called recently, and she was also upset that Nancy had not wanted to deal with an irate creditor who was chasing payment for an account.

So I knew when Nancy came to me that, indeed, Nina was not pleased with Nancy. What I then had to do was to deal with this situation, resolve it, and help to mend the relationship; otherwise Nancy's pleasure at work would remain significantly diminished, and so would her performance.

I asked Nina if she was willing to meet with Nancy and me, and she agreed. We made a time and got together. Firstly, I asked both Nancy and Nina whether it was important for the two of them to work together effectively. Both said it was important, and that their effectiveness was definitely better if their team work was good. Thus, we established an agreement that good teamwork was wanted by both of them.

I then asked Nancy to tell me what she was feeling, rather than telling me about a series of incidents. To her credit, Nancy clearly expressed that she was feeling ostracised by Nina, that Nina did not want to have much to do with her, that Nina was being very cool toward her. Nancy also said she wanted to know from Nina what had happened to cause this change of relationship.

My strategy in situations like this is to use a 'garbage dump' process.

All of us, through our lives, have gathered together a set of experiences that can colloquially be described as our 'baggage.' This baggage resides in our subconscious minds, and is the cause of much of our responses to situations that confront us. The garbage dump process is designed to recognize and to dump some of this baggage, so that we can get on with our lives! The more unhelpful baggage we are able to leave behind, the easier it is to move forward.

In the context of relationships, this baggage can becomes like a wall between human beings. Each episode or experience with another human being that upsets us is like an additional piece of rock that piles up. After a while, if the pile of rocks is not cleared, or dumped, it can permanently block and destroy the relationship. Unfortunately, it is sometimes very difficult to clear because we tend to believe that we are right and the other person is wrong, and our egos get in the way of taking the first step to deal with the upsets, or the baggage.

The key to the garbage dumping is to have the courage to tell the truth about our feelings. When we express our feelings, by the use of 'I' messages, the response from the other person is usually most heartwarming. The use of the 'I' word is critical to the process. In the case of Nancy, she could have started out by saying that Nina was being a bitch to her, or was being unfair, or something along those lines. The powerfully effective alternative, which Nancy used at my request, was to say clearly 'I am feeling hurt and rejected.' It is not difficult to imagine which of the two strategies above would evoke an even more productive response in Nina.

Nina responded in an open and nondefensive way. She had the courage to say to Nancy: '…I was feeling upset and angry because you could not be bothered finding me when my husband rang, and on top of that, you refused to take the phone call from the creditor when I asked you. What was particularly upsetting was that this is an important part of your job as receptionist, and you were with one of your girlfriends talking about office chairs and ergonomics.'

Here was the answer to the breakdown of the relationship. Nancy and Nina had a totally different perspective of the same set of events.

How often is this the case in our relationships? Aren't most difficulties caused through these different perspectives, which arise because each of us has a uniquely different set of filters through which we experience life? These filters reside in our subconscious minds. It is only through clarity in our communications with another human being that the different perspectives can be appreciated and then resolved. Unless one person allows another a different perspective, then the chances of a real relationship are almost minimal.

Nancy's perspectives on the issues raised by Nina were quite different. We explored them. I played the role of mediator, and made sure that neither of them accused the other of anything. Nancy felt unable to take the call from the creditor because she was talking not to a friend of hers but to an acquaintance: an ergonomics expert who had given her time to check why Nancy was having shoulder problems. Nancy could not remember the time that she had failed to put Nina's husband's call through to her, but on exploration it appeared that Nancy had made a simple mistake: she'd been distracted from passing on the message due to a staff member's birthday cake arriving at the office at the time of the call.

When Nina heard Nancy's perspective, having already expressed with clarity and courage what she'd been feeling, all of the baggage between them dissipated almost miraculously, and the energy between them reverted to the warmth that both of them wanted.

It has been my experience that most people want to have warm and caring relationships. Given the choice, not many people that I know would choose poor relationships, or conflictive relationships. The problem seems to be that not many of us have clear and simple strategies for removing the baggage or rubbish that gets in the way.

With Nancy and Nina feeling warmth toward each other again, the opportunity arose to capitalize on their expressed desires to work together as a team in the most effective way possible. I asked Nancy whether she was willing to accept ideas and suggestions from Nina on better and more effective ways to fulfil her role as receptionist, without feeling that each idea was a criticism. Nina had been with H Corporation for six and a half years, so her awareness of better ways of doing things was quite high.

Nancy agreed with this, and the meeting ended with Nancy and Nina resolving to sit down together with Glenda, Nina's assistant, to work out better ways of tackling their respective roles and the achievement of better work practices. A little while later, as a consequence of these discussions, Nina was appointed office manager, to be the team leader of the three of them and ensure that the team really worked as a team.

In summary, through the garbage dump process, the relationship between Nancy and Nina had been improved, and Nancy's level of enjoyment increased significantly. Obviously, so did her ongoing contribution.

So what is your organization's attitude to relationships? Is it consistent with your own? Or is it one that treats such issues as unimportant? Any significant mismatch will steal your passion, your drive and your motivation. Your awareness of this mismatch becomes a significant clue for you.

What would you do to change such an attitude in your organisation? It is worth digressing to deal with this.

CHANGING THE ATTITUDES IN YOUR WORKPLACE

Assume that the leader agrees with you that relationships are important and that at the present time relationships are not very good. This is the first step: the leader has to agree that there must be a change! Without that commitment, just forget it, and either leave that organization or choose not to care about the relationship issue.

I believe that the two keys to relationships in the workplace are trust and a commitment to our co-workers. Another way of saying this, which I tend to avoid in first meetings, is that the two keys are trust and caring or love. (This last word is a little too threatening to the business world, and I don't want the message to be lost in the anxiety or fear that is created when the word *love* is used.)

Here are the relationship building blocks that will create results for individuals in an organization and thus for the organization that they work for:

- Great relationships require trust and commitment between the people to each other.
- An environment for building trust will be generated if the people forming the relationship accept that they are working for essentially similar goals.
- People are more likely to be committed to each other if they are working for similar goals.
- Individuals need to commit to their organization's purpose, vision, goals and values.
- Individuals will be able to commit fully to the organization's purpose, vision, goals and values if that commitment is congruent with the attainment of the individual's own purpose, vision, goals and values.
- The individual will need to become aware of his or her own purpose, vision, goals and values before making a commitment to them.

The challenge is to find out what our purpose, vision, goals, and values are. This process requires a significant investment of time and effort which, far from receiving encouragement in our Western world systems, is usually greeted with cries of 'narcissism,' 'belly watching,' and 'mid-life crisis.' In my experience with the corporate programs I have participated in, and facilitated with many of the highly regarded businesses in Australia, very few people are able to articulate what they want.

So how can they commit to their goals when they do not have any? And if they do not have goals, imagine how hard it is for them to commit to the goals of their organization. This failure to know oneself, and then to commit, lies at the heart of many of the relationship difficulties in the workplace. It is immensely challenging to create trust between people who suspect that everyone has his or her own individual agenda.

The first step for a leader is to understand the above process, and to create the purpose, vision, and goals for the organization that is both inspirational for those who work there, and possibly congruent with the usually unconscious purpose, vision, and goals of the individuals. I have found that it is not strictly necessary to identify individual goals before creating the organization's goals. However, the more numerous the people who can participate in and contribute to the articulation of the purpose, vision, and goals, the greater its power.

To then create an environment in which trust and commitment to one another can flourish, the goals and vision must be disseminated throughout the various teams, and the commitment of individuals must be sought. This process of commitment to a common goal and vision is the oil that facilitates smoother interrelationships, and the glue that keeps a team together. This is so because individuals start to sense that they are each working for the common good, which also has benefits for individuals. If each person can sense that others want similar outcomes, that they are marching in the same direction to the same tune, it is much easier to want to relate to those other people.

On the other hand, how could you expect trust and commitment to flourish in a 'dog-eat-dog' environment, where our futures are dependent on 'beating' the other people in the organization, where another person's success necessarily means your prospects for success are diminished? That is the dilemma of business in the twenty-first century, and very few organizations deal with the dilemma successfully.

MISTAKES

Your organization's attitude to mistakes has a significant impact on you and on your level of passion! This impact is so important that I shall deal with the issue in the next chapter.

PERSONAL DEVELOPMENT PROGRAMS

Many people have said to me during programs that I have facilitated that they do not know what they are passionate about, they do not know what they want to do, they do not know what they love doing, or, at the very least, even if they do know what they love to do, they believe that it is unrealistic to expect to earn a living from doing it. My response to them is to ask them what structured process or strategy they have undertaken to find their passion.

Finding your passion is like finding what you are capable of on the athletic field: unless you have a go, and unless you put your body, mind, and soul on the line, you simply will not achieve what you are capable of achieving. Our Olympic heroes of all descriptions have gone through massive hardships, effort, and pain, and have applied huge commitment and discipline to fulfill their dreams. They almost always need to exercise great courage not to give up.

What are you willing to do to find your passion? Remember, this issue was discussed at the start of the book: unless you can see and feel the benefits of finding your passion, then you are unlikely to take any difficult, or apparently difficult, steps which involve pain!

There are structured means that you can follow to find your passion. Personal development programs are a great way to begin; if you have started in this way and have not found what you are looking for, then keep going. Persistence is the vital ingredient! In any event, even if you have not found your passion, your participation in the courses is still teaching you very valuable lessons.

Just ask yourself whether there is a program that you have attended that did not teach you *anything*.

Let me summarize the personal development path I have taken, including structured courses, which directly and indirectly have led me to writing this book:

- My first intuitive response is to mention Father Zoltan Varga, a Jesuit Priest, who had a close association with my parents and family. Father Varga was my first philosophy teacher, and I did not avoid the opportunities he gave me to discuss my life and the 'big' questions.
- I attended an Edward De Bono seminar in 1979. While I was always a creative thinker, de Bono expanded for me the possibilities of different ways of thinking, and of different perspectives available on almost every issue.
- I read a large number of books on alternative ways of

living, particularly my father's library. My father has always been willing to stretch the limits and think laterally. His library includes an extraordinary range of material on physical and metaphysical issues. On the physical side, his alternative thinking led to the establishment of Kovess Organics in 1976, and the acquisition of our family farm at that time for the purpose of producing our own organic foods.

- I was given a copy of Michael Gerber's video, *The E-Myth*, and then acquired Gerber's book. This led me to reevaluate the way I practiced law, and to become aware of the possibilities for radically altering the way in which law is practiced in all of Australia! I received this video for my 40th birthday, in 1992, and I now see how the video laid the groundwork for my departure from the law.

- In November 1992, one month after receiving the Gerber video, I attended a course called 'Money and You,' a program that ran for three full days. This course was an extraordinary and enlightening experience that introduced me to the life and work of Buckminster Fuller. It also introduced me to Robert Kiyosaki, the author of a most worthwhile books, *If You Want to be Rich and Happy, Don't Go to School*. Robert has subsequently achieved worldwide seccess with his book *Rich Dad, Poor Dad* and *Cashflow Quadrant*.

- In February 1993, I began a ten-week course called 'Mastery,' a follow-up program to 'Money and You.'

- In May 1993, I traveled to Hawaii to attend the Excelerated Learning Institute's 'Business School for

Entrepreneurs,' a further extension of 'Money and You.' This 16-day program, conducted at an intense, frantic pace using accelerated learning techniques, is said to be the equivalent of a standard MBA conducted over 12 months. What I learned during this program led me, on my return to Melbourne, to resign from the practice of the law as a solicitor and start my career as a professional speaker, workshop facilitator, and executive coach.

- In August 1993, I attended a six-day intensive program called 'Super Teaching,' a program designed to develop 'super' teachers who are willing to put their hearts and minds into effectively transferring information. This course challenged many aspects of me, and led to numerous, valuable discoveries about how I function as a human being, and the impact that my fears have upon me. I shared a room with Jim Stynes, one of the best Australian Rules football players, whom I had met some months previously. Jim's motivation for his footballing success is an inspiring story, well told in his book *Whatever it Takes*.

- In September 1993, I attended a weekend course called 'Beyond Self-Awareness,' conducted by two experts in Neurolinguistic Programming, Wyatt Woodsmall and Marvin Oka. This course, too, challenged me to explore myself more deeply. It reinforced for me, like the preceding courses, that 'all answers lie within.'

- I undertook Neurolinguistic Programming studies over the period from August 1993 through December 1993, using the course materials developed by Dr. Tad James that Jenny used as part of her NLP qualifications.

- In February 1994, I attended a weekend workshop on Buckminster Fuller, conducted by Jerry Speiser in Melbourne, called 'The Future by Design.' Fuller's views on how our Spaceship Earth (a phrase he invented) should function for the maximum benefit of all of us have been a powerful guide for me in all aspects of my people development business; indeed, in all of my life. One of his views, as expounded in his book *Critical Path*, is that '... human continuance now depends entirely upon the intuitive wisdom of each and every individual...'

- In October 1994, I attended Anthony Robbins' one-day program entitled 'Strategic Influence,' a wonderful learning experience about human behavior, and my first direct experience of one of the world's best speakers in the field of personal development. Robbins is a personal coach and mentor to many leaders around the world, including former President Bill Clinton and tennis great Andre Agassi.

- In April 1995, I attended two courses over a period of one week, with two experts in music and touch, Ardie and Jack Wilken. These courses introduced me to a new understanding of my feelings, of my sexuality, and of the ways to access parts of me that I did not know existed. It also taught me new ways to appreciate the impact of music on human beings, which was both beneficial and also surprising, since I have been playing the double bass in bands and orchestras for almost 25 years.

- Between April 1993, and May 1995 I continued with my study of myself through the ongoing practical implementation of many of the techniques I had learned from the above programs, as well as practicing the techniques taught to me by Yvonne Evans, my then business partner. These exercises were challenging, confronting, and scary, and required ongoing courage to be willing to expose the parts of me that I felt were nothing to be proud of, that I had spent most of my life hiding from the view of my friends and acquaintances.

These techniques included:

- Time Line Therapy
- Aromatherapy
- Hawaiian huna
- Yoga
- Channelling of information
- Neurolinguistic Programming
- Massage
- Reiki

- In May–June 1995, I completed a ten-week course, of two hours each week, in reevaluation counseling. This was challenging, and taught me a process of getting in touch with my feelings and 'discharging' the emotion trapped in my cellular memory. The key skill that I developed was the ability to listen actively and to assist the person I was counseling by asking good questions.

- In July 1995, I attended Anthony Robbins's weekend program 'Unleash the Power Within' in Sydney. The significant positive influence of my lessons from this program are with me every day! While experiencing the exhilaration of overcoming fear and completing my first 'firewalk experience,' I also learned the process of how to alter beliefs that prevent me from achieving my goals.

• In February 1996, I attended a ten-week program of the Melbourne School of Philosophy, which was an introduction to philosophy. The most memorable aspect of this program, which explored many alternative philosophies, was that 'philosophy' is the love of, and search for, wisdom, and that wisdom can be attained only after we know ourselves. Thus, the message keeps recurring: when each of us seeks to understands himself or herself, and through this process finds his or her passion, then we can start to understand what our lives are about!

• From March 1996 through to October 1996, I undertook a Postural Integration Program with a master practitioner in that field, Robert Young. This program was designed to help balance my mind-body-spirit aspects, using various techniques including shiatsu massage.

• In March 1997, I attended a weekend program entitled 'The Breakthrough Experience,' a program developed by Dr. John Demartini of the USA. The 'collapse technique' that is demonstrated and experienced in that program is unique and valuable, and is well described in Demartini's book *Count Your Blessings*.

I have never attended a course that, at its conclusion, I judged to have wasted any of my time or money—and I have invested many thousands of dollars in cash and time in pursuing the above path to self-awareness. I am proud of the fact that I was willing to do this, to keep learning, to keep stretching my reality, to constantly create new realities, to exercise the courage to keep expanding my awareness and my consciousness.

So, what is available for you now, if you were willing to start a structured process for discovering your passion? Here are some suggestions. I do not recommend any particular programs over any others; I am simply bringing to your attention some of the courses and programs that are presently available in Australia. Many of the programs are available in other countries. When you begin to attend some of these programs, you will be guided in your next steps. In other words, once you are 'in the game,' the opportunities for your ongoing learning will keep coming, just when you need them, if you keep your mind open to them.

Possibilities are:

- Alpha Dynamics programs
- The Cairnmillar Institute programs in Australia
- Dale Carnegie Training Programs
- Effective Leadership International (a course designed to enhance your personal and leadership skills through self-knowledge)
- Excalibur Program
- Hoffman Process
- Insight Training Seminars (experiential learning programs designed to enhance the quality of your personal and professional life)
- Landmark Forum Programs
- Martial arts of any description. I have been exposed to Tai Chi, Aikido, Tae Kwon Do, and Kung Fu. From my limited knowledge, I believe that most master practitioners of martial arts include elements of mind/body/spirit in their

programs, and the experienced practitioners that I
have spoken to all claim that their self-awareness
grew immensely through martial arts.

- Meditation centers such as Sri Chimnoy Centers,
  and the Brahma Kumaris Raja Yoga Centers. Raja
  Yoga is described as a pure form of meditation
  which blends a unique spiritual education with
  open-eyed meditation. The Brahma Kumaris also
  conduct the World Spiritual University. Another
  valuable meditation centre is conducted by Ian
  Gawler in Victoria, Australia.

- Neurolinguistic Programming. These courses provide valuable insights into human behavior, and
  particularly our own behavior. In other words,
  through such courses we can become consciously
  aware of how and why we behave in particular
  ways. Why is conscious awareness relevant? The
  best metaphor I have found is that 'it is hard to
  pull the weeds out of the garden unless you are
  aware that the weeds are there!'

- One-on-one counseling with your favorite counselor. If you do not know any counselors, just start
  asking your friends: you will be amazed at how
  many of them already spend time with counselors;
  they will be able to guide you in your choice.

- Phoenix Rising Workshop, a weekend program
  presented by Graeme and Gayle O'Brien.

- Postural Integration Program. This is a type of body-
  work that deals with the entire self, the unity of
  every part of the body, the outside together with the

inside, and the unity of our bodies with our minds and our spirits. It works on the basis that, as we change old, rigid body postures, we need also to change the accompanying rigid feelings and thought processes; or if we release blocked emotions and ideas, we need to free simultaneously the muscles and tissues for new, more flexible movements.

- Rebirthing centers.
- Reevaluation counseling, a program that teaches you to be a counselor at the same time as being counseled. It is a useful way to get in touch with your feelings, instead of suppressing them.
- Reiki courses. Reiki is a powerful yet gentle form of 'hands-on healing' which practitioners achieve by their ability to access universal life force energy. Learning to become a Reiki practitioner creates a significantly expanded awareness.
- Anthony Robbins' programs of any description (particularly 'Unleash the Power Within,' which includes a firewalk experience)
- SEEK International (especially for children and teenagers)
- Shaolin Kung Fu. a branch of the martial arts taught by my friend Robert Z.; see his Website: **www.shaolin.com.au.**
- Silva Mind Control Method. This program teaches specific mental techniques that can put you in touch with your feelings and allow you to take responsibility for them and your direction in life.

- Soul Centred Psychotherapy conducted by the Kairos Centre in Melbourne. This is a three-year part-time program. Its basis rests in teaching ways to attend to each person's unique process of inner work, so that value and meaning emerge from within.

- Switch on Success with Sandy McGregor. Programs that teach scientifically proven techniques that 'unleash the other 88% power of your amazing mind.'

- Xeros, formerly known as 'People Knowhow,' which conducts a number of courses, the foundation course being 'The Turning Point.'

- Finally, read, read, and read some more! Anything that appeals to you in the 'self-help' field will almost certainly be of value.

The above are simply some guidelines. The list is certainly not exhaustive, and while I have had experience of many of the above, I have not attended them all. I have spoken to people who have attended each of the above programs, and none of those people told me that they regretted attending the programs. What the list gives you is a starting point. I would be amazed if, after reading the list, you could honestly say that you do not know where to start a structured approach to finding your passion.

Let me add a note of warning and of hope. Many people attend programs such as those listed above, and then find, some months later, that apparently nothing has changed in their lives. To their dismay, and chagrin, they also find that other participants in the relevant programs have had major, positive changes in their lives as a direct consequence of the programs. In these circumstances, it is possible to feel somewhat of a failure, that 'there must be something wrong with me.'

I encourage you to be aware of this syndrome and to allow and acknowledge that every program will have a different effect on each and every participant. This book is about finding your uniqueness; it makes good sense that programs will have unique impacts on each participant and that your experience and benefit is not a function of whether you are good, bad, or anything else.

The hopeful part is that whatever effect any program has on you, it is a fact that your commitment to implementing the lessons and insights from the program will determine the ongoing benefits. That is, the more you practice, the better you will become at whatever it is you want. If you do not practice, you will forget much of what you learned in the program.

In my own case, for almost two years on a daily basis, I have been practising techniques that I learned while attending Anthony Robbins's 'Unleash the Power Within' program. The longer I practice these techniques (which, among other things, include a process of changing my limiting beliefs), the more fulfilled I find myself to be!

Jack Nicklaus, one of the world's greatest golfers, is quoted as having said: 'The harder I practice, the luckier I get.' I would rephrase this to read: 'The harder I practice, the better I feel!'

KEY POINTS FOR CHAPTER 2

- Review the subheads in this chapter.
- Identify the issues that stop you from finding your passion.
- Start keeping your 'Passion Diary.'
- Adopt the saying: 'What other people think of me is none of my business.'
- Review the 'coincidences' in your life and identify the patterns.
- Accept that you will need to access your courage to change anything in your life.
- When vulnerability meets vulnerability, you will create intimacy: be vulnerable!
- Personal development programs are a great starting point in the quest to find your passion.

CHAPTER 3
The Value of Mistakes

CHAPTER 3
The Value of Mistakes

'Good judgment comes from experience;
Experience comes from bad judgment.'

— **Author unknown**

*E*mployees often complain that they are put down in front of others for making mistakes. As I stated earlier, times are changing at an ever-increasing pace, and one result is that our opportunities for making mistakes will continue to increase. We will make more mistakes because both the future and human behavior are becoming less predictable, and because the information age and the technology explosion means that much of our information is changing by the second.

Let us consider how these factors will lead to us to making mistakes. The Internet is a topical example. The explosive growth of interest in, and use of, the Internet in the mid to late 1990s was unpredicted by many, including Microsoft's Bill Gates. Suddenly, the daily news media contained detailed discussions on how 'electronic commerce,' or buying products and services over the Internet, would be the next great sales and marketing opportunity. Many companies acted accordingly, and spent millions of dollars to exploit the opportunity. Alas, the pundits were mistaken, and very few companies, in both the Australian and American media, have reported profitable results from this new medium.

Here is another example. The information age enables us to be informed about new products and services which appear in any part of the world within a few minutes of their release to the public, where some years ago it would have taken some months to become aware of the details. Suddenly, the 'great new idea' is copied by competitors, and millions of dollars are invested, through the mistaken belief that the media hype will guarantee success in their relevant markets. However, despite the product's benefits, even newer or different products emerge within a very short period of time, and the public's interest in the first idea dissipates at a far rapid rate than used to be the case twenty years ago. Two specific industries where this happens is in computers, and in fashion, both men's and ladies.

Why are mistakes valuable? What is the attitude in your organization to mistakes? If you believe—quite rightly, as we shall see—that mistakes are valuable because they are learning experiences, and yet your organization punishes its people for the mistakes they make, you are likely to be frustrated and unhappy about people being publicly criticized for their mistakes. You will not expand to your true potential in such an environment.

Becoming aware of this issue could lead you to urge a change in your organization's culture to appreciate the value of mistakes. Alternatively, your increased awareness could lead you to find another organization to which you wish to contribute your passion and energy, one that understands the value of mistakes. And your increased awareness would help you to identify the appropriate organization and to effectively investigate its values around mistakes.

I have made lots of mistakes. I have made mistakes with my clients. I made a mistake when I lost half a million dollars on a couple of business deals that I did not discuss with my wife. I made other mistakes that cost my firm large amounts of money, I made mistakes when I gave clients credit, and I made mistakes when I was interpreting my behavior. One of the most valuable lessons that I have learned as a result has been to understand exactly what these mistakes were and the exact nature of my reaction to them.

Mistakes are valuable. I know that intellectually, and yet I still feel anxiety about some of my actions. This anxiety reinforces for me the way that our subconscious minds function: it does not matter that we *know* or **understand** something intellectually; if mistakes in the past have been painful emotional experiences, the anxiety can still surface.

After much soul-searching, I became aware that my anxiety about mistakes was created by my well-intentioned parents and care givers. The overwhelmingly unanimous advice from all of them throughout most of my infancy and childhood was that if I did not make mistakes I was a 'good' boy and therefore lovable, but that if I did not do the right thing, if I made mistakes, then I was a 'bad' boy and much less lovable.

Since a withdrawal of love is probably the most painful emotional experience that can be imposed on a child, it is no surprise to me that my 'stuff' comes up around the issue of mistakes. I have learned to use the word *stuff* through the personal development programs that I have attended. It is a nonthreatening, slightly humorous way of describing the responses and reactions that arise from our subconscious minds, particularly the upsetting or negative types of responses.

So, how do we handle and change this type of unhelpful, subconscious response? As an example, let me take you through my own journey of self-discovery and changing of behaviour. I believe it will be helpful, because the principles are applicable to any issues that block you from pursuing your passion—issues such as fear of rejection, fear of disapproval, fear of loss of security, and so on. These are the steps that I took in my journey, in order:

- an understanding of how my subconscious mind works
- an awareness that the particular anxiety I was feeling related to a fear of making mistakes (This was quite difficult to arrive at.)
- an intellectual exploration of the whole subject of mistakes, leading to an understanding of their value
- a process of linking massive pain to future anxiety and linking massive pleasure to a willingness to act and make mistakes
- practicing making decisions and facing the risk of making mistakes (This was based on my strong belief that practice makes better, and the more practice I am willing to undertake, the less my anxiety will be.)

We have already explored aspects of the first two points, so let us deal with the intellectual aspects of understanding, and appreciating, the value of mistakes. No one has addressed the issue any better, in my view, than Buckminster Fuller, who wrote:

By cosmic designing wisdom we are all born naked, help-less for months, and though superbly equipped cerebrally, utterly lacking in experience, ergo utterly ignorant. We were also endowed with hunger, thirst, curiosity, and procreative urge. We were designed predominantly of water—which freezes, boils, and evaporates within a minuscule tempera-ture range…

Under all the foregoing conditions, whatever humans have learned had to be learned as a consequence only of trial-and-error experience. Humans have learned only through mistakes. The billions of humans in history have had to make quadrillions of mistakes to have arrived at the state where we now have 150,000 common words to iden-tify that many unique and only metaphysically compre-hendible nuances of experience. The number of words in the dictionary will always multiply as we experience the progressive complex of cosmic episodes of scenario uni-verse, making many new mistakes within the new set of unfamiliar circumstances…

Those quadrillions of mistakes were the price paid by humanity for its surprising competence as presently accrued synergetically, for the first time in history, to cope success-fully on behalf of all humanity with all problems of physi-cally healthy survival, enlightening growth, and initiative accommodation.

Chagrin and mortification caused by their progressively self-discovered quadrillions of errors would long ago have given humanity such an inferiority complex that it would have become too discouraged to continue with the life expe-rience. To avoid such a proclivity, humans were designedly given pride, vanity and inventive memory, which, all togeth-er, can and usually do incline us to self-deception.

Witnessing the mistakes of others, the preconditioned crowd, reflexing, says, 'Why did that individual make such a stupid mistake? We knew the answer all the time.' So effec-tive has been the nonthinking, group deceit of humanity that it now says, 'Nobody should make mistakes,' and pun-ishes people for making mistakes. In love-generated fear for their children's future life in days beyond their own survival, parents train their children to avoid making mistakes lest they be put at a social disadvantage.

Thus humanity has developed a comprehensive, mutual self-deception and has made the total mistake of not per-ceiving that realistic thinking accrues only after mistake making, which is the cosmic wisdom's most cogent way of teaching each of us how to carry on. It is only at the moment of humans' realistic admissions to selves of having made a mistake that they are closest to that mysterious integrity gov-erning the universe. Only then are humans able to free themselves of the misconceptions that have brought about their mistakes.*

Bucky Fuller can be a pretty forbidding type of writer to understand, so let me put these ideas in a different way.

Human beings learn fundamentally through trial and error. Children are intuitively 'hungry' to learn; they devour opportunities to do new things. However, our Western education system promotes the concept of 'getting the right answer.' And both adults and today's students are 'punished' for getting the wrong answer. That punishment takes the form of being laughed at in the classroom, or getting bad reports, as we have seen.

Many organizations pay lip service to the concept of valuing mistakes as a learning experience, but the truth is that the penalty paid within those organizations for making mistakes is large indeed. It is very similar to our classroom experiences. This price, as showed by employees in programs and workshops, can be:

- loss of face
- humiliation
- demotion
- embarrassment
- criticism
- loss of self-esteem

Here we are, at the beginning of the twenty-first century, in an extraordinary time of change, when none of us is able to predict the future, and yet we want to punish our people for learning! What a waste of opportunity!

The key to creating a learning, and therefore, a successful, organization is to understand the value of mistakes. If mistakes are valued, only then will the lessons from them be adopted and implemented by the organization. Only then will they be handled openly, shared, and the lesson spread to others.

We have often heard talk of 'empowering' an organization's people. This can only happen if these people are willing to take risks. Risk-taking necessarily increases the chances of making mistakes, but if the negativity attached to mistakes is not changed, then no empowerment can occur. Unfortunately, such negativity is deeply ingrained;

it lies in our subconscious minds, where, despite our conscious desire to change our responses, the fear of mistakes remains a powerful force.

That is why it is so difficult to create a learning organization, to empower individuals, and to aim for the model (developed by W. Edwards Deming) of the constantly improving organization, which led to the concept of total quality management.

The solution, in my experience, is first to value mistakes, then to make a commitment to change the philosophy of the the organization throughout. That change will need constant reinforcement and repetition. Understanding the value of mistakes will also help to give you the courage to pursue the difficult and potentially threatening process of changing your organization. The philosophy will change only if the leaders are willing to be real leaders and to take risks themselves. If the leaders won't take risks, why would the followers?

So what has all this got to do with passion? It is about recognizing the issues or behaviors that can 'kill' you on the inside. Mistakes are such a natural part of our existence that it is impossible to avoid them. Yet, if our work environment forces us to avoid making mistakes, we will need to act unnaturally. Under such circumstances, it would not be surprising if our passion for work were to desert us.

Your greatest defense against such a scenario is to develop awareness of what is going on inside you. One effective way of doing this is to practice meditation. Learn to recognize what happens when you, or others, are trying to do your best and you feel rising inside you the familiar pressure that indicates fear of a mistake.

Another defense is to understand *why* the leader of your organization has a need to put people down or criticize them when mistakes are made. In some cases this is the leader's own inner critic speaking, the manifestation of an internal dialogue in which he criticizes himself when he makes a mistake. Let me quote from a letter I wrote to one of my clients after a team building workshop:

Dear Geoff [not his name],

After our recent meeting, we have taken some time to think through the discussion we had with you regarding the future decision-making process at your company and the choices that are open to you for future action.

Our perception of your current frustration at your company revolves around the issue of 'getting more out of your staff,' to increase productivity and achieve budgets. You also want to feel confident that you have a 'motivated' team on deck with a good measure.

Our suggestion at the time was to further address the current staff members' capacities for improvement by firstly changing the style of encouragement that you give each team member to increase their confidence levels and provide them with a core level need. Simple as it sounds, addressing a core level need in an individual is the key to producing real growth in the business and greater profits. You will get more out of your team if you address core level needs!

An alternative solution could be to change some of the team members in order to increase productivity and contribution levels; the premise behind this being that new people who are 'go-getters' will automatically improve productivity levels and not require any change in leadership style regarding encouragement factors.

At first glance, this can seem the smartest logical step. With a closer look, however, we find that this is rarely the case.

What commonly occurs in this scenario is that the original dynamics simply repeat themselves. That is, we unconsciously hire individuals who have core level needs that we later ignore. So what happens is that the new team members start off okay (new job, new impetus, etc.) but eventually they too move into the groove of the unconscious dynamics in the organisation and their performance and productivity slip.

The key to your company lies in you.

You are the person who controls the dynamics of your company. Our experience with leaders is that the very thing the team needs at a core level, in order to improve their confidence, initiative and motivation, is the one thing that the leader needs and denies giving to him- or herself. Your 'internal voice' speaks to you in a harsh, judgmental manner and is not an encouraging voice at all. The person at your company who is hardest on themselves is YOU!

Our suggestion would be for you to start talking to yourself in a less harsh manner, with some kinder comments and encouraging acknowledgments for yourself. Put aside the weirdness of our suggestion, and start being kind to yourself. As you become more self-supportive you can then become more staff-supportive.

We know you feel that they get enough encouragement, but we sincerely feel that your view on this is clouded by a history of not receiving enough encouragement yourself. We would love to see a situation in which you 'overdose' yourself on positive reinforcement. It is truly amazing how powerful it is to focus on positive, encouraging points of view. There is a library full of research to verify this fact. Positivity has a precessional effect: positive increases in profits, positive increases in productivity and performance and positive increases in job satisfaction!

Any team leader who wishes to:

- increase each individual's effort and productivity
- maintain a motivated team
- create and sustain initiative among the individual

and the team members must first discover the core key need of the team, and the core key need within him- or herself, AND SATISFY THAT NEED. At your company the key need is encouragement and recognition. This needs to begin within yourself: encourage and recognise YOU and allow yourself to hear encouragement and recognition from those close to you. No one else need be aware of this approach unless you choose to discuss it with them.

Then gradually begin to give the same encouragement out to your staff, ESPECIALLY DURING THE

TIMES WHEN THEIR PRODUCTIVITY HAS DROPPED. This is when they REALLY NEED IT. And our guess is that this is when YOU really need it also.

As that Japanese man in the Mitsubishi automobile advertisements says: 'Please consider.'

I have quoted the entire letter here because it goes to the heart of what happens when self-criticism transfers to criticism of others. It took me some courage to analyze my client's problem so bluntly, because I felt a little worried that he would not like what I said. Fortunately, the client recognized the truth, and has been working on the issue ever since.

Is the pain you feel when you or others are put down for making mistakes enough to generate or support the courage to speak your truth about mistakes? If so, you will take steps to change your organization, or get out of that environment. Recognizing such pain becomes a most valuable clue for you in identifying one of the suppressors of your passion.

* Fuller, B. 'Mistake Mystique,' in *East West*, April 1977, pp. 26–9

KEY POINTS FOR CHAPTER 3

- The more mistakes you make, the wealthier you are!
- Human beings are designed to learn only through trial and error.
- Identify your own fears of making mistakes so that you can overcome them.
- Making mistakes helps to keep you relevant for an ever-changing business world.
- Great businesses value the mistakes of their employees.

CHAPTER 4
The Need for Introspection

CHAPTER 4
The Need for Introspection

'Only I can change my life.
No one can do it for me.'

— **Carol Burnett**

$\mathcal{A}$ few years ago the Australian government set up an Industry Task Force on Leadership and Management Skills to research and report on the creation of leaders and managers into the twenty-first century in Australia. Its findings were published in 1995 as the 'Karpin Report.'

It began with these words from the chairman to the Minister for Employment, Education, and Training:

Following almost three years of consultations, research, study missions, and analysis the Task Force has prepared a report which provides the most comprehensive insight ever into the way Australia prepares its managers for work and leadership. It also presents policy recommendations and options based on Task Force findings.

The improvement in the performance of Australia's managers is an important complement to the government's wide-ranging microeconomic reform, export enhancement and workforce training initiatives.

The report proper went on to say:

...Economic improvement cannot be separated from social development, nor efficiency from equity. Increased employment, effective diversity management and cultural change are about people and community. Team skills, communication and employee development are about better working lives and satisfaction for individuals.

The Karpin Report identified the number one failing of our present leaders and managers as a lack of people skills! What are these people skills? How are they defined? They are the linchpin of what this book is about.

The key to development of people skills is a deeper understanding of yourself; the more you explore and understand yourself, the greater your ability to understand others. People are more than their thoughts, and it is necessary to get past their thoughts, into their feelings and into their spirit, to appreciate the complex creation that is the human being. Without an understanding of human complexity, our people skills will be very limited indeed.

The first step toward a deeper understanding of ourselves is to take a good look inside—to practice 'introspection.' Introspection leads to awareness. By way of illustration, let me tell you about my introspection journey, which was one of the factors, and part of the process, that caused me to give up being a successful lawyer and to commence a new career as a professional speaker, workshop facilitator, and executive coach.

MY INTROSPECTION JOURNEY

When I look back on my life, I often 'think' that I made many wise decisions, or that 'coincidences' which impacted upon me were simply just that, coincidences. As time passes, I am becoming increasingly aware of all the influences which came upon me and now realize that 'I did not consciously decide that,' or that an event was not a simple 'coincidence': that is how my spirit or soul wanted it to be! Taking the time to practice introspection gave me this insight, and being aware that my soul impacts on my decisions and the events which occur in my life gives me an ongoing sense of comfort, of an ability to accept an event that is happening to me, even when I may *think* that the event is a negative one.

From the age of ten I had a job delivering morning newspapers. I did this because I came from a financially struggling family of six children (I was the second oldest), and because I wanted to generate my own money. Through the experience of delivering newspapers, I met a lawyer, Stuart Purnell, as already mentioned. His firm was called Morrison Teare and Purnell.

At that time, in 1963, Stuart was about 53 years old. I was 11, and had wanted to be a lawyer since I was 6. There was no conscious intention on my part to meet this man, who practiced as a solicitor, and who took a wonderful, fatherly, mentor-type interest in me and my future life.

My parents, who were born in Hungary and came to Australia three years before I was born, were both telling me that I could not be a lawyer because there were no jobs for children of Hungarian migrants, that it was virtually impossible for a migrant child to succeed in such an 'establishment' profession. That was their perception of the legal job market at that time.

Stuart's 'coincidental' encouragement in the opposite direction was therefore pivotal. When I was completing matriculation, the final year of secondary school in Victoria at that time, Stuart Purnell paid me a lump sum that enabled me to 'retire' from my paper route. Not having to get up at 5:30 A.M., I could concentrate on my study.

Stuart and I had built such a relationship over three years that it was obvious that I was going to work for him. I completed matriculation in December 1969 and started in Stuart's law office the next day. My career in the law, including university studies, extended over a period of almost 24 years. Throughout my four years of university study, I spent every holiday break working full time with Stuart, then completed my Articles of Clerkship with him—a year of on-the-job training that is compulsory before one can be admitted as a solicitor. This was a man who had no vested interest in me, and the question intrigues me to this day: What is it that made Stuart Purnell do what he did?

The next pivotal 'coincidental' relationship in my life was one I developed with Neil Young QC, later to become chairman of the Victorian Bar Council (the barristers' organisation). I met Neil in February 1970 at a pre-university camp, and we spent many fun times together.

In the first two years and my first eight subjects, I passed all subjects and I was awarded two honors. Then Neil showed me how to approach the study of law, which he had worked out for himself (our university lecturers, alas, did not teach us such things). By using Neil's approach, and with no extra work, I gained eight honors in the eight subjects I studied in the final two years of my degree! As a result I graduated with an honors Degree in Law.

(I still find it extraordinary that students in law school are not taught how to study law! Certainly, they are taught what to study, and what they need to know, but not the most effective and efficient ways to achieve the goals of the law course. My own experience with my schooling, and the schooling of my four children, is that few of us were taught the processes of learning and thinking. And yet these are the very processes that Edward de Bono has spent 30 years encouraging educational establishments to teach! Changing any system continues to be a drama! Vested interests are as difficult to shift as our existing behaviors. But I digress…)

The next 'coincidence' occurred in 1974 when Neil Young was completing his Articles at Mallesons, then Melbourne's largest law firm. At the end of my Articles, Stuart Purnell told me I was most welcome to continue working with him, but he knew that I really wanted to practice tax law. I wanted to practice tax law because I knew the people with tax problems could afford to pay my fees, that I would not have to go through the anxiety of charging people who really had problems and who could not afford to pay me.

So I talked to Neil Young and he suggested that I ring Matt Walsh, one of the partners at Mallesons. I did not know Matt Walsh, and so wrote a letter to him and expressed the desire to work with him. He rang me the next day and we met with Max Ham, one of the firm's senior partners. The next day, which was Saturday, unbeknown to Matt, a large advertisement appeared in the *Age* newspaper:

'Mallesons, Solicitors wanted.'

While Matt and Max had made up their minds on the Friday to employ me, they rang me on the Monday to say that they were a little embarrassed, that they did not know that their partners had decided to advertise.

Having placed the advertisement, the partners felt obliged to put me through the selection process. However, Matt Walsh attended the interview with me and answered many of his partners' questions on my behalf! It would have been interesting to see, had I not taken the initiative, whether I would have been employed, given that there were hundreds of responses to the advertisement. To this day, I am amazed at the 'coincidental' timing of my decision that led to the writing of my letter to Matt Walsh.

Some three years later, it was time for the next 'coincidence.' In 1978 I was playing A-grade water-polo and was President of the Lorne Surf Life Saving Club. One of the members of the Club, Don McDonald, was a personnel consultant, a 'headhunter.' A client of Don's, Alan Vorrath, who was working with a lawyer, Garrick Gray, was also a former water-polo colleague of mine from university days. Alan was seeking an experienced tax lawyer.

At that time, I had been at Mallesons for three and a

half years, and my career was progressing steadily. I was earning $15,000 per annum and was rendering fees to clients at a multiple of ten times my salary, when the acceptable rule of thumb for a good employee solicitor was a multiple of three times (and still is today). I was achieving this level of performance at the most expensive law firm in Melbourne, and Mallesons did not even have a system to know where clients came from or who was responsible for bringing them to the firm!

After I left Mallesons and reviewed all the work that I had done in the years that I had spent there, I realized that I had attracted 40 percent of the clients. While the firm gave me the other 60 percent, to a large extent it was my network of friends and connections that enabled me to generate fees of ten times my salary. In hindsight, it was poor management not to have a system to identify my client-generating and income-generating ability.

The legal partners Alan Vorrath and Garrick Gray were keen for me to join them, and offered me a salary of $50,000. I did not immediately say yes, so Garrick increased the offer to $100,000! My salary was to be increased more than sixfold and I would have the opportunity to continue to practice in the area of law I enjoyed most. How could I resist?

After discussing my future career prospects with Matt Walsh, I accepted this offer that had come up 'coincidentally' in my life. Had I chosen to stay at Mallesons, I have no doubt that I would have become a partner of the firm, I would probably still be there, and you would not be reading this book.

Some 18 months later, on May 1, 1980, I established my own law firm and conducted a successful practice for the next six years. On May 1, 1986, I merged Charles Kovess & Co with Barker Harty (now known as Barker Gosling). Was it 'coincidental' that these events occurred on May 1? I practiced at Barker Gosling for seven years, became head of the commercial law department, and was involved with expanding the firm nationally. On June 15, 1993, after some philosophical differences with my partners, I decided it was time to share the power of passion on a full-time basis.

Throughout my legal career many other things happened to me that I now realize were not consciously organised by me. When I look back at how it unfolded, I *thought* I was in control, I *thought* I was making many wise decisions, and yet all these *coincidences* continued to have a massive impact on me.

Over that period of time, as well as law, I was involved with football, including being part of the 1974 A Grade premiership with University Blacks in Amateur Australian Rules Football. I also won a number of Victorian championships in surf life saving, qualified as an international water-polo referee, became chairman of the Victorian Water Polo Association, and maintained an extensive involvement in groups of people in community and school organizations, including five years' presidency of St. Roch's School, which was attended by each of my four children.

During my involvement in all these activities, I realized that very few of the people that I was interacting with were doing what they wanted to do, what they loved to do, or what they were inspired to do.

During the 1980s, I was secretary of the University of Melbourne Law Society, comprised of graduates of the law school, and spent some time with Professor Michael Crommelin, dean of the law school. I was also a member of the Legal Education Committee of the Law Institute of Victoria. It became apparent to me that many young students were taking up the study of law because they'd achieved excellent results in their final year of schooling, and had *qualified* for law school. It was also apparent to Australia's law schools, and the Melbourne University Law School in particular, that many of these students did not particularly *want* to practice law; yet they did not know what they *did* want! The message that such students seemed to be responding to was, and still is, that entering the legal profession is a good way to make significant amounts of money!

Professor Crommelin knows that he does not want the law school dominated by the pupils who got the best marks in their final year of school, yet no practical alternative is being used to decide who should be admitted to the law school when applicants far outnumber the available positions. It is a dilemma exacerbated by the fact that many of the great lawyers in Victoria over the last 50 years only became lawyers because they were returned servicemen from World War II! After the war, the Australian government instituted a scheme whereby returned servicemen could attend university and study whatever course they chose. I know a number of such lawyers, and they have assured me that they would never have qualified for law school in the competitive environment that existed even then! And yet, these people made great contributions in the legal profession without being academically outstanding.

The conclusion I draw from the above is that academic excellence is not necessarily the key to success in the legal profession, nor, indeed, in any profession. I am sure that the leaders of university departments also believe this, but our system offers very little room to maneuver outside the scores generated by the school system. Recently, however, there is evidence that some tertiary education institutions are implementing practical ways to address this problem. The Royal Melbourne Institute of Technology requires prospective architecture students to 'prove' their desire to study architecture through the production of a reasonably extensive portfolio of drawings prepared by those prospective students. Some medical schools now include surgical procedures in the first year of the course, to 'weed out' those students who cannot cope with blood.

Of course, you the reader will not be surprised by my assertion that the key to success in any calling is the level of passion that is devoted to the calling, or the extent to which the person is passionate about the calling. As I have stated earlier, our education system is not geared to assist help students find, then pursue, their passion.

Our students are being told today, as I was told in the 1960s, to study hard, and to get into the habit of studying hard, so that they can score good results. They are being given this message very early in school life. Why are they being given this message?

One key reason is that when they are studying their final year, they can score a great mark. They are told that it is critically important to score well, because it is critically important to their futures, and specifically important to help them 'get a job.'

In my view, the philosophy behind such a message is flawed and my opposition to it is one of my reasons for writing this book. This unfortunate message is also disseminated by politicians: Senator David Kemp, then Minister for Education in the Australian Parliament, publicly stated that his government's educational policies are worthy ones because they 'will help young people get jobs'! I reject the philosophy that the key purpose of educating young people is to enable them to 'get a job,' and the sooner this philosophy changes, the sooner we can deal with the fact that, significant numbers of people under 25 years of age are unemployed.

You may ask, if getting a job is not the major purpose, of education, then what is? There are many alternatives to the educational model that is currently in vogue in Australia—and, it seems, in much of the Western world. I believe that education should be a process in which each unique human being is taught various strategies that could lead to the development of the full potential of that human being. I am all in favor of education, but it is more than *data*, it is more than *research*, it is more than *intellect*.

Education must encompass and encourage *inspiration*, *passion* and *soul*, and must include what Daniel Goleman in the title to his best-selling book calls *Emotional Intelligence*. Students in our education system must be given the opportunity to discover their passion. It is not true today to tell students, that gaining good marks in school is the key ingredient to success: it is simply *one* of the ingredients, and the problem is that focussing on the marks means that *many other* essential ingredients are ignored. (By the way, by 'successful,' I mean nothing other than a person achieving the 'success' that that person wants. Success, in my view, is entirely subjective: no one is capable of telling another person what success is, or imposing some type of objective definition of it on others.) Consequently, and consistently with the views in this book, i say that gaining good marks in the final year of school is not the only way to be successful.

So when I left Barker Gosling in 1993, I had to decide whether I would stay in the law or whether I would pursue this issue of passion. I was passionate about the law, I remain passionate about the law, I loved being part of the legal profession, but I came to the realization that what I am more passionate about is passion itself and the importance of each one of us following our passion.

In early 1993, I 'coincidentally' met Yvonne Evans, who was doing some counseling work with my children. I took the opportunity at that time to extend my knowledge of myself, including the way I was interacting with my children. (I thought I knew how to handle people until I had children! How many of us parents are capable of managing our children?)

I was having difficulties in understanding how best to relate to Rebecca, my eldest child and only daughter, and Yvonne was helping me with that process. Because of my training and experience as a lawyer, when Rebecca said she was feeling 'bad,' my question would inevitably be 'why'? Automatically, albeit unknowingly, I was requiring her to justify to me why she was feeling bad, and if she gave me a reason that I thought was inappropriate, I would immediately but unintentionally criticise her by saying 'You shouldn't be feeling like that!'

Yvonne helped me see that a far more useful question was not 'why are you feeling like that?,' but 'what exactly are you feeling?' That is, 'describe what you are feeling.' This was such a significant and useful shift in my thinking that I was simply amazed, and was left wondering 'How long has this been going on? How long have I not known this?'

I realized that, throughout my twenty-four years in the law, dealing with people, leading teams, handling people, handling committees, I had not ever become aware of this apparently simple issue! This new awareness which arose out of my introspection journey was instrumental in leading me to leave the law and establish Kovess Evans Training & Development Pty Ltd with Yvonne (Yvonne has since left, and the company is now called Kovess International Training & Development Pty Ltd.) The key philosophy behind the company's work in the corporate field is to 'access the passion of employees to generate outstanding results, through bridging the heart and the mind.'

Yvonne's talents were very different to mine. By teaming up a left-brain-thinking, logical, reasoning person who had practiced as a lawyer with a behavioral counselor and therapist who had behavior science training, people training and spiritual training, and who used right-brain skills such as intuition, feelings, and creativity, we forged a successful business partnership.

And the alliance was even more valuable because

accessing this powerful resource known as 'passion' is a *process*, not just a simple few steps. It was Yvonne's skills and 13 years of learning, coupled with my understanding of business and life, and my residual passion for the practice of law, that not only enabled us to create the company but, specifically, to develop a program for lawyers called 'Rekindle Your Passion for the Law.'

My company has subsequently presented similar programs to organizations such as the Commonwealth Bank, National Australia Bank, ANZ Bank, Telstra, accounting firms, real estate firms, government departments, and Essendon Football Club. When dealing with groups of people, we do not teach them customer service, we do not teach how to implement particular software programs. What we deal with is the people issues in the organization, and how to change the environment and the corporate philosophy so that it serves those people better, so that they want to contribute, and do contribute, more of themselves to the organization. They will do so because they become passionate about the work that they are doing. It is my belief that, if the people issues are handled more effectively, the company will improve its performance. Indeed, I believe that the *only* way to achieve outstanding performance in business is by helping the people access their passion through accessing their minds, their bodies, and their souls.

During my 20 years in the legal profession, practicing business and corporate law, very few lawyers and business leaders that I met appeared to understand what these people issues were about, just as I had not understood the effect on my daughter when I asked her to justify or prove to me why she was feeling as she did, effectively laying down rules on how she was allowed to feel.

When leaders decide that they want to access the talents of the people in their organization, then introspection by those leaders is a powerfully effective way to commence that process. I repeat: your ability to understand another person is a function of how much you understand yourself, and introspection increases your understanding of yourself.

The August 22, 1994 edition of *Fortune* magazine contained a wonderful, inspiring article by Stratford Sherman entitled 'The Voice Within,' and discussed the relevance of introspection to business, management, and leadership. I made a note of several important points in the article, and I would like to share these with you:

> Executives generally aren't an introspective lot, but in the dawn of the New Economy—with no job security or clear career path, with more responsibility and less certainty than ever—stressed-out managers increasingly are turning inside for answers.

> Business schools from Harvard to the University of Southern California are including in required course work exercises in reflection. Mainstream corporations such as AT&T, PepsiCo, Hoechst Celanese, and Aetna are integrating various forms of introspection training into management development programs.

> Is the new introspection a fad? Of course it is—but this may be the healthiest fad in years. To the degree that individuals are successful at plumbing their depths, those people should be better off, and the companies that employ

them may gain competitive advantage. In fast-shifting markets, the unexamined life becomes a liability. 'The old management paradigm has run out of steam... This company is not going to be successful unless we have people who can learn from experience...We need our people to act independently, to be accountable and responsible for managing their own piece of the business. It takes a certain amount of reflection to do that successfully.'

Organizational change begins with leaders who walk the talk by transforming themselves. As winning companies find they must engage workers' hearts as well as their minds, this increasingly emotional aspect of business is destroying the old corporate machismo that once allowed us to keep our feelings hidden and our inner lives mysterious, even to ourselves.

I was delighted that *Fortune* was reinforcing the main concept behind my new career—that inner exploration of deeper issues at the individual level is the key to the future in business! However, I was moved to write at that time to the editor, in the following terms:

> Dear Sir,
> Your article in the August 22, 1994 edition on the critical importance of leaders learning to heed 'the voice within' was timely and wonderful, but Stratford Sherman did himself a disservice by describing the introspection process as a 'fad.' I feel he wanted to keep on-side with the cynics, who like to rule through fear, and who think that being in touch with self is only for the wimps.

Well, two geniuses, 2000 years apart, prove to me that introspection, or whatever we want to call the process of understanding ourselves, is no fad: Jesus Christ, who taught that 'the kingdom of God lies within us,' and Buckminster Fuller, who in his foreword to his seminal work, *Critical Path*, wrote:

'...I am convinced that human continuance now depends entirely upon:

• The intuitive wisdom of each and every individual...

• The individual's integrity of speaking and acting only on the individual's own within-self-intuited and reasoned initiative...'

Our training work gets results because we focus on the *individual*, and when the individual is in touch with himself, the promises of Christ and Fuller are fulfilled: the true brilliance of the individual can be uncovered, and the contribution to the organisation becomes extraordinary.

Yours faithfully,

Charles B. Kovess

Therefore, I encourage you to continue with, and expand, your introspection journey, and inspire those around you to do the same. Introspection will occur when you participate in personal development courses. Introspection will help you to understand yourself better and will help you to access your passion. When you grasp the benefits of introspection for your life, you will not be concerned about the views of others who may think that you are simply pursuing the latest management fad, and you will simply do it! If you need to convince your boss, or those to whom you answer, that the process is valuable, be aware that your ability to convert someone to your point of view is a function of your beliefs. I will expand on this issue in a later chapter.

I have mentioned the need to take risks to follow your passion. It is possible that the introspection process will cause you to take risks. I took a risk in leaving the legal profession, particularly a financial one. At times, the going was tough, and doubts crept in. Gabriella Lang unwittingly, and 'coincidentally,' appeared at just the right time.

I sent to to Gabriella Lang a copy of my company's newsletter. I had met Gabriella while I was practicing law, and she was working for Rosemary Howell in a legal personnel consultancy. A few days later, I received the following response:

> I received your newsletter the other day—thank you for thinking of me.
>
> I have been meaning to let you know what has been going on in my life since we spoke on the phone; was it almost two years ago?
>
> Well, like you, I have decided to 'follow my passion' and given up the law and am engaged in writing my doctoral thesis—on Russian history of all things. The noise you hear as you read this comes from several generations of Hungarian ancestors rolling in their respective graves at the thought!!
>
> Although it was a very difficult decision to give up paid employment and return to full-time study, I have not looked back, and can honestly say it is one of the best things I have ever done. As well as researching for my Ph.D., I am also learning the Russian language as it is essential that I be able to read relevant documents in their

original form. This has been immensely challenging, but great fun and in June/July this year (1996), I spent 6 weeks in St. Petersburg and Moscow—fascinating but hard work!

During this period, I managed to fulfil two long-held dreams. I have been obsessed by Russian history for as long as I can remember and as a child, I always used to say that one day I would go to 'St Petersburg.' Well, thanks to the amazing changes which have taken place in that country, I was able to do just this! And while I was doing research in the state archive in Moscow, I was actually able to hold the diary of Tsar Nicholas II in my hand!!! (The way this came about is a long story, suffice to say that $50 can get you just about anything in Russia these days!!)

I wanted to tell you this as I know that you are in the business of telling people to follow their dreams, and for me, it has been an incredible experience.

Well, Charles, I hope that your company continues to go from strength to strength. If you are ever in Sydney, please contact me—if you have a free evening, we would love to have you and your wife come to our home for dinner.

Regards and best wishes,

Gabriella Lang

This letter, unsolicited as it was, arrived in early October 1996. It made my heart jump, and gave me an incredibly warm feeling. Sometimes, I would find myself wondering whether I could make it financially, having left my legal partnership that had been generating a significant income, and going through the hard times of establishing my credibility in a new career. Gabriella's letter was like a message from my spirit to hang in there, even though it is tough, because the results will come and my derams and goals will be achieved.

So the effect that my newsletter had on Gabriella in causing her to write was a reminder that my work was indeed having an impact.

Of course, there is a valid view that making an impact should not matter, that so long as I was following my heart, nothing else mattered. However, one of my core values is to 'make a difference' to our planet. I must admit that receiving one letter from Gabriella made me believe that many other people must have received a positive benefit from the newsletter without necessarily feeling the need to write.

It is gifts such as this letter that are one of the inspiring, unexpected and exciting rewards which the passionate life produces!

KEY POINTS FOR CHAPTER 4

- The more you understand yourself through introspection, the more you are able to understand others.
- The key to success in business is to harness the unique potential of each person.
- If you are passionate about your work, you'll never work another day in your life.
- Allow for the possibility that your soul may have a different agenda for you than your mind.
- Academic excellence is not the key to success in business.
- The purpose of education is not to just 'get a job.'
- Accept that each person is uniquely different in many, many ways: this will increase your tolerance levels.

CHAPTER 5

The Importance of Values

CHAPTER 5
The Importance of Values

'Follow your bliss.'

— Joseph Campbell

If you are in business, you have probably attended a number of training and development programs in your career. Some programs would have been more effective and helpful than others. And I would not be surprised if the ones you found the least helpful were those that failed to address the question of human values.

In the programs I have presented over a number of years, almost all participants admit that they have not 'gotten around' to discovering, let alone listing, their values. Yet I do believe that you can net even begin to understand your behavior until you become aware of your values.

WHAT ARE 'VALUES'?

Each of us has a set of standards, or measures by which we run our lives. Our standards may differ from those of others in certain ways and be similar in other ways. Often, we can live our lives from day to day with scant awareness of what our standards are and how they influence our choices, decisions and effectiveness. Yet these standards, which are closely aligned to our life's experiences (starting from birth), are what give us our 'values'— our sense of what is important and worthwhile for us in our lives. Your values guide your decision-making processes, regardless of whether you are consciously aware of your values or not. When you know what is most important to you, making a decision can become much simpler.

CLARIFYING OUR PERSONAL VALUES

So where do you start in working out what your values are? To assist you in this process, I will list a number of values. All you have to do is to mark the 10 to 15 that are most important to you. While you may believe that most of these values are important to you, the fact is that some are more important than others.

POSSIBLE VALUES

Love	Courage	Determination	Perseverance
Persistence	Success	Dedication	Loyalty
Commitment	Freedom	Passion	Challenge
Competition	Prosperity	Innovation	Health
Stability	Conformity	Contribution	Comfort
Impact	Personal growth	Growth	Achievement
Caring	Accomplishment	Intimacy	Power
Control	Being fit	Happiness	Friendship
Inspiring others	Fun	Vitality	Warmth
Intelligence	Excitement	Investing	Creativity

Cheerfulness	Trust	Intuition	Being the Best
Acceptance	Excellence	Harmony	Respect
Gratitude	Relationship	Recognition	Wealth
Learning	Intimacy	Pride	Discipline
Confidence	Strength	Flexibility	Self-esteem
Adventure	Integrity	Honesty	Choice
Equality	Hard work	Importance of Team	Individuality
Sense of community	Simplicity	Group versus the individual	
Ability to contribute	Making a Difference		

When you have decided the most important values for you personally, it is valuable to put your values in order—or, in other words, to decide upon your scale, or hierarchy, of values. The relative importance to you of each of your values is what you use to make any decision. When you are having difficulty making decisions, it's wise to check the issues involved in the decision against your scale of values.

An everyday demonstration of the importance of knowing your a scale of values is the conflict that many of us have in deciding between 'health' and 'wealth.' Here is a process that I use in our programs. I ask: 'Are you as fit and healthy as you want to be?' The answer is overwhelmingly 'No.' Then I ask: 'Which is more important to you, "wealth" or "health"?' The answer is overwhelmingly 'health.'

But when I press for reasons why people's 'health' is not as good as they would like, I am told that demands in the workplace limit the time available for health and fitness.

In other words, many of us sacrifice our health for our financial well-being! Or, put another way, while we *say* that health is more important than wealth, *in practice* we seem to sacrifice our health for our wealth!

Have you taken the time to discover your values? If not, why not? Could it be because you have not clearly seen the significant benefits that would accrue if you did so? Let's have a look at the main benefits.

The Benefits of Knowing Our Values

In business literature and personal development programs, there is much talk about the need to set goals. Yet success in achieving goals is only possible if the goals we set are in alignment with our values. And we cannot possibly bring about such an alignment if we don't know what our values are. Hence, the achievement of goals is the first benefit you stand to gain from clarifying your values. Ask yourself two key questions: What values should you eliminate from your list in order to achieve your ultimate outcomes, your life's purpose? In what order do your values need to be to achieve your outcomes?

A second benefit is that, by becoming *consciously* aware of your values, you will be equipped to change your behavior so that it is congruent with your values, with what is really important to you. This is a very empowering stage of development to reach; it is like being told that to reduce your cholesterol levels, you must not drink whole milk. When you know what needs to be done, your ability to do it is enhanced.

A third benefit is that you will be able to discern whether your values are in alignment with the values of the organization that employs you, or the organization that you lead. If the values are not in alignment, the internal conflict for you can be severe, and will rob you of much of your potential. I explored this aspect in earlier chapters. However, when there is alignment, the energy flow within you is not blocked, and your ability to be inspired becomes available.

PASSION AND SIMPLICITY

Recently, there have been several articles in newspapers and magazines dealing with the concept of 'voluntary simplicity.' This process involves the decision to simplify one's life, to 'turn on, tune in, drop out,' to rid oneself of all unnecessary aspects, including goods and chattels, friends, mortgages, and other obligations and responsibilities.

If simplicity is an important value for you, discovering your passion, and then pursuing it, will be a critical guidepost. You cannot decide what is unnecessary until you become aware of who you are and what you want.

Unnecessary complexity comes into our lives because of our search for fulfillment: we have not been encouraged to be ourselves, to find ourselves. We have been taught that the acquisition of objects is the key to fulfillment and to happiness, that we are successful when we have more objects.

While this may be so for some people, and I am certainly not judging whether this is good or bad, you know whether the pain of your life to date is being rewarded with the pleasure of fulfillment and nourishment. If your pleasure is insufficient, find your passion, discover your values, and then you will have a much greater ability to discard what is unnecessary in your life!

PERSONAL AND WORKPLACE VALUES

Once you have determined your values and their hierarchy, you can then decide whether your values are in alignment with those in your workplace. If your values are significantly different from those in your organization, then you will find it difficult to be fulfilled, to be inspired, to be motivated, to be passionate about your work.

One example of an area with potential for a conflict of values is, as we saw earlier, when professional firms render fees on the basis of time recorded on jobs. While time may be spent on a matter, a person's effectiveness, and therefore the value to the client, may well be misrepresented by the time spent. The professional has actually spent the time, but if honesty, were practiced, the client would not be charged for the full amount of time. The actual time spent on the jobs is consistent with the need to generate fees, and accordingly to create wealth. The final choice between 'honesty' to the client and 'wealth' to the firm involves a value judgment.

If your organization does not have clearly enunciated values, then I would encourage you to take responsibility for discovering them and making everyone aware of them! Even unenunciated values do nevertheless exist and govern behavior unconsciously. Let me now take you through a practical process that is used, to help people find their values.

On a sheet of paper write the heading 'What Is My Life Composed of Now.' Under the heading draw a word picture of yourself. Do this by listing all the issues that you are dealing with in your life right now. Draw your life, including work, your relationships, your family, your creativity, your growth and everything else that is important to you. Do this in map format, with lines leading out and with labels for all of the different aspects that apply to your life.

Remember that there aren't any right ways to do this drawing, and if it feels incomplete, maybe that is significant. Just draw and write what *feels* appropriate, what *feels* right for you at this time, because that will give you clues about what is going on inside you. Think back to this as you finish reading this book, then fill it out a little more.

Below is a list of some issues that you might like to consider in relation to your life. Do you feel a lack in any of these areas?

Health	Loving relationships	Children and family
Business	Work	Money
Play	Study	Personal growth
Intimacy	Unity	Re-creation

(I have deliberately hyphenated the last one—'re-creation'—because recreation is often about re-creating things. When we have recreation with our family, we are re-creating family. When we are having recreation with our partners, we are actually re-creating a partnership, we are re-coupling.)

If any of these areas strike you as being deficient in your life, highlight them with a marker pen. Mark the ones where you have the sense, 'I have not quite got what I want there.' For example, 'I have not quite got great health... I have not quite got the intimacy I want... I am not really sure I am growing and developing.'

It is very important that you be honest; otherwise you are only cheating yourself. So if you have to highlight the lot of them, then highlight the lot of them, because this could be a real turning point in your life, a turning point in your awareness. After that, look at the following different ways of feeling, different 'states' that you can feel:

- peace
- passion
- relaxation
- a sense of challenge
- a sense of curiosity
- feeling of contemplation
- reflectiveness
- feeling of expansion, a feeling that there is so much to move into and experience.

Highlight those that you feel you have achieved, as well as those that you wish you had. Then complete the statement 'My life is in need of...'

Refer back to these particular aspects or areas, then go back to your picture. Have a look at it and reflect on it for a moment. Ask yourself 'Well, what is missing there?' You can get a significantly heightened awareness sometimes, by going back and looking at your picture.

I notice, when I go through this process with people in our programs, that most of the aspects of many people's lives are on one side, clearly demonstrating a lack of balance; or, the picture is often 'top heavy,' indicating that there are so many 'neck up' aspects going on, and a lot of burden around the shoulders. Other areas are often left quite blank, and for some people the picture is quite balanced.

When you discover what is missing, you can then go out and create it. But if we do not make the time to discover what is missing, then we do not know. We are just too busy, we are just being swept along with all of our 'doings.' It reminds me of that classic concept: 'We are so busy doing it, doing it, doing it, that we have hardly got an opportunity to be!' I am well aware of this dilemma: in my past, I judged my self-worth as a function of what I was *doing*. I now find it helpful to constantly remind myself: 'You are a human *being*, not a human *doing*!'

At the end of this process during a workshop, when I ask participants to complete the statement 'My life is in need of…,' I ask whether anyone wants to share a particular insight, or whether anyone has a real eye opener that surprises them or something of which they had not been aware of.

One participant once answered, 'For me, I think it is all those things that you mentioned in the list: the 'peace' through to the 'expansion.' Some concepts have more importance than others, but I think all of those words apply to what is missing for me.'

As a specific example, I have found that most legal practices are very stiff environments, a very restrictive environments, very 'left-brain' environment, where values that are shown on the list—peace, passion, creativity, relaxation, challenge, curiosity, enthusiasm, joy, contemplation, and expansion—are almost necessarily excluded from the workplace. It is almost mandatory that, if you go into law, you can forget many of the values on the list, with the exception of a hell of a lot of challenge.

A participant in a workshop for lawyers once said in completing his picture:

> My health could be improved if I lost a couple of kilos in weight. I do not relax enough and I do not get much time to contemplate but I still, I think, experience most of those things starting from 'peace.'
>
> However, I am not sure what you mean by 'passion.' Just looking at all these states of mind, it just seems to me that the practicing of law has probably changed my personality to some extent. Someone just said 'immensely,' and I think it has changed immensely
>
> These states of mind are the sort of things you have when you are young and the loss of them is probably just life doing this to us generally, regardless of whether I am in or out of the legal profession. But I just think my own personality, in terms of being introverted and quieter than usual, I think it has certainly had an effect on me.

My co-presenter in this seminar, Yvonne Evans responded as follows:

> Yes, I think you are right. My brother is a carpenter by trade. He works with his hands, and he's a beautiful, fun-loving sensitive guy. All my memories with Mark are of laughing at Marx Brothers tapes and we just seemed to laugh all the time. Then he had a wife and

two children, and the building industry went under, so he took a job as a warder in Pentridge.

Mark's initial training occurred in H Division and for four years I watched him change. He got through the shock of the first few months, although it was pretty horrific for him, and then bit by bit I started forgetting what he used to be like. His new behavior became the norm. Then he quit 12 months ago and went back into the building industry.

I went to visit him, and realised that here was my brother back again. I mean, I had tears in my eyes because I had forgotten, I did not realise the 'real' Mark had gone and had now returned! These work environments that we put ourselves into have this gradual chip and knock effect, they just gradually chip away at you. So I think you are right. And recently, I have been around lawyers through being in business with Charles and it seems that nearly everybody is saying the same thing that you are, John, that our real selves are disappearing under the strain.

So I am wondering what is keeping this system going when so many people are really disillusioned. So, our outcome for all of you, from today's program, would be for you to get closer in touch with the 'real' you, and look at perhaps what is not helping you to flourish to be the real you. You know that different plants need different spots in the garden: some need the sun in the morning, some need the sun in the afternoon, some need watering every day, some need it once a month and so on... Then you have the unique little gems, the really exotic plants that need constant and unusual car.

Often we can discover when doing these processes that there is a part of us that needs that special care and attention and we really have not had time to give them to ourselves. These special needs are what give you your uniqueness and give you your color and yet, from the time when we move through our education system and suffer cruelty from our peers for being different in any way, we seek to conform and to avoid any chance of being ostracized for our differences!

As Stuart Purnell, my mentor, used to tell me:

The children who have the best time at school are the average children, the children who do not stand out. The geniuses, the slow ones, the thin ones, and the fat ones, they're the ones who are made to suffer! They are different from the gang!

Some of us used to suffer, and our children still suffer, these experiences of being told 'you're the dumbest, you're the slowest, you're the fastest…,' and the little light in us that is so unique starts to get dimmer and dimmer and dimmer. It is a conditioning process where we all start to look the same, sound the same, so that we are not ostracised, so that we are welcomed by others.

Oh yes, we can pretend in certain areas that we are a little bit different, but really, at a core level, we have been educated to hide that core unique essence that makes us truly different. Our passion comes from this uniqueness, and this is why we can so easily lose passion, forget what it was, and just do what our peers and our elders tell us is 'practical, and realistic, and the best thing for you!'

This book, and the programs we run are about helping people to rediscover their unique attributes, to put passion back into their lives and the lives of the people with whom they relate—about expanding their ability to achieve whatever their unique real selves may want to contribute, in whatever job or industry they choose. Understanding values is a critically important part of this rediscovery process.

KEY POINTS FOR CHAPTER 5

- Review the subheads in this chapter.
- Writing down your scale, or hierarchy, of values helps you find your passion.
- Once you know your values, you can then write down your goals.
- Knowing your values helps you to identify any behaviors you need to change.
- Align your values with the values in your workplace to nurture your passion.
- Knowing your values helps you to avoid unnecessary clutter in your life: life becomes simpler.

CHAPTER 6
Passionate Employees

CHAPTER 6
Passionate Employees

*'Nothing is really work,
unless you would rather be
doing something else.'*

— James Matthew Barrie

*P*assionate employees have an impact on the success of any business, and in every case that impact is far greater than is visible or provable. None of us can ever be fully aware of the impact of our words, our deeds, our spirit, and our energy. What we can be aware of is that this is the case and that the greater the passion of a person, the greater the impact.

Human beings are designed to be a balanced unity of mind, body, and spirit, and passion comes from our spirit, from our soul, from our heart. When an employee is passionate, all three aspects of the employee are engaged and are used by the employee in his or her role. Each employee's role varies during the course of every working day. Even the most mind-numbing process worker's job contains different elements. If you do not believe this, consider the impact that such a process worker in, say, the food industry, can have on the marketing success of the business in two different circumstances:

- The worker tells all of his friends that his work-place is the cleanest and friendliest that he has ever experienced.

Or,

- The worker tells all of his friends that his work-place is dirty and unhygienic and that the managers are interested only in maximizing profits, with little regard to anything else.

You can readily see that the worker's role is broader than just doing the mind-numbing task.

The impact that employees can have is in direct proportion to the extent to which all three aspects of their humanness are involved. My picture of what I am trying to express is that of a circle, split into three equal parts. When you take away one or two of the parts, the circle becomes an irregular shape and also becomes smaller. The smaller the shape, the lesser the impact. The bigger the circle, and the more rounded the circle, the greater the impact. In the realm of physics and the laws of gravity, Newton discovered that the greater a body's mass, the greater its gravitational attraction. The moon circles the Earth, because the Earth has a greater mass than the moon. The Earth circles the sun because the sun's mass is greater than the Earth's. This principle is the same in the metaphysical world, in the world of mutual attraction between people and products and services, and is consistent with the laws of nature.

Passionate employees have a greater sense of themselves, of their self-worth, and even have greater self-confidence. They *feel* bigger because all three of their aspects are engaged. They know how powerful and effective they can be in the workplace, so they are less fearful of losing their jobs: they know they can make a contribution in many different environments. Therefore, they are less fearful of being themselves, they are less likely to seek approval, they have little fear of being rejected and so are more able to face the risk of rejection, and they are more likely to tell the truth as they see and experience it.

Among the types of impact that passionate employees have are that they can:

- make customers want to do business with you
- make people want to become customers
- make customers become part of your sales and marketing, because they are so impressed that they tell all of their friends
- make the workplace a challenging, exciting environment
- promote innovation and experimentation
- refuse to leave when they are offered more money by a competitor
- be more likely to tell the truth, so that decisions that need to be made by leaders for the future are based more on fact than fiction
- inspire loyalty amongst other staff
- *want* to relate to their colleagues and therefore increase the likelihood of great teamwork.

Every business to which I have consulted, every business that I personally know, and every business that I have read about wants to have the above-listed dynamics working in their organization, yet very few manage to achieve even a small number of them.

In Australia and in the United States, significant numbers of new businesses fail within the first five years of establishment. My view is that a business with more than a few of the above attributes will not fall within this depressing and challenging group. However, since so few employees seem to be passionate about their work anyway, the failure role seems to me to be consistent with the philosophy that motivated me to write this book: **unless** employees are passionate, the chances of a business failing are greatly increased! The message in this chapter applies to both employees and employers: both groups have a vested interest in the ongoing success of the business.

THE IMPACT OF PASSION ON CUSTOMERS

I have worked on people issues with a successful Australian men's clothing chain, 'Gaz Man,' owned by Garry Austin. The company has twenty of its own retail outlets and also supplies as a wholesaler to other menswear retailers. It is in an extremely competitive, mature industry. One of the keys to its ongoing success is the quality of the experience that customers have whenever they walk into a Gaz Man store, particularly in terms of the way that the store manager and other employees relate to the customers.

The way that human beings relate to each other is a function of how much of us is *present*, how much of our three aspects are engaged at the point of relationship. If the Gaz Man retail employees are passionate about the business, their spirits are present, their hearts are involved and they become more attractive to the customers, the customers *feel* like relating to them, and the quality of communication improves dramatically. Of course, the customers are not the only ones to benefit: the employees' level of pleasure rises because of the quality of the communication and the relationships. In this way, customers feel safe, they feel it is okay to rely upon the employees in terms of the products and styles that they may be buying, and the whole buying experience becomes joyful and uplifting.

I am sure that all of you have experienced the type of interaction I have just described, but my own experience in Australia and overseas is that this happens in a minority of instances. The more a business can achieve quality communication with its customers, the more likely it is that those customers will return. And passionate employees will be much more likely to achieve these levels of communication.

There is another critical reason why the quality of communication is so important: most customers cannot distinguish between the quality of a product that they buy from Gaz Man or any other business and most of the competitors within the relevant industry! For example, most clients cannot:

- differentiate between the skill levels of lawyers, accountants, doctors, and dentists

- differentiate between the quality of motor vehicles, or other common household goods, in a similar price range
- distinguish the differences in the products of competing financial services businesses.

In contrast, I suggest that people make the decision to spend their money based upon criteria *other than* the alleged quality of the particular product or service, and that one of the key issues is the quality of their interaction with the employees of the business with which they are about to transact.

Customers who are delighted with dealing with your business, with dealing with you, will not easily leave you. They begin to trust you. You make their lives more simple, you make their lives less disordered, you make their lives less unpredictable for just a short period of time.

Michael Gerber, in his wonderful book *The E-Myth*, discusses the McDonald's Corporation and calls it the world's most successful food business. Gerber's book had a major impact on me, and I had the pleasure subsequently of meeting him and spending almost an hour 'shooting the breeze' with him, as well as attending one of his seminars. Gerber's key message is to work 'on your business and not in it,' which means the need to develop *systems* that will achieve desired outcomes, so that the proprietor's attendance at the business is optional. He claims, and I agree with him, that people go to McDonald's for their food because the experience is predictable—it is the same *every single time*!

If customers can rely on your employees, or on you if you are an employee, if they can trust, then they will be much more likely to remain your loyal customers. They will tell their friends and acquaintances about you and they will be keen to help you succeed in your business. They will give you referrals, they will give you ongoing valuable feedback on your failures and mistakes, and they will become part of your market research team when they tell you what your competitors are doing to try to attract them away from you.

Beliefs are also a critical issue in the performance of employees. I have adopted, for use in all of my training programs, a sentence of six words, which I first heard from an American financial planner, Nick Murray. It is:

'When I believe, I am believed.'

The psychological issues that lie behind this seemingly simple sentence are profound. Our beliefs create our individual destinies. Knowledge of our beliefs, and an ability to change them, are both important aspects of our respective journeys. If employees are not passionate, their level of belief in the product or service of the business is likely to be low. If they have a low level of belief, any customers that they relate to will tend to adopt a similar level of belief. The best example of this is the case of the salesperson. The more she *believes* in the product she is selling, the greater will be her ability to sell, and the greater the *passion* she has for the business she represents, the higher the level of her *belief* about it and its products.

Therefore, be aware of what your employees believe about your business and about its products and services. Be aware of what you believe about your job, about your leaders, about the staff you manage. These beliefs will determine your success.

CHALLENGE AND EXCITEMENT
IN THE WORKPLACE

For a business to prosper sustainably in the existing world circumstances, it must be a challenging and exciting working environment. As Bob Dylan wrote, 'The times they are a-changing.' The adjustments that are needed to cope with external change will not happen in a dull workplace, the necessary personal and technical skills development of employees will not occur in an unchallenging workplace. Challenge and excitement will keep employees vital and motivated because they will be aware of the attendant growth opportunities for themselves, particularly when the leaders have an enlightened practical philosophy about the need for, and the value of, mistakes.

Passionate employees will know this, they will not be frightened of demanding the changes that will help the business to prosper, they will not be fearful of confronting the leaders and managers and expressing their views on what is at stake when challenge and excitement are missing.

PASSION, INNOVATION, AND
EXPERIMENTATION

Managing the Innovating Enterprise: Australian companies competing with the world's best is the 1993 report on a study commissioned by the Business Council of Australia and chaired by Sir Roderick Carnegie. The report is valuable and contains useful examples and insights. One of these is:

Unlocking the creativity of the people in the workplace is a key source of improvement. This is one of the reasons why employee relations is so important to developing an innovating culture...The best enterprises unite their people around a common purpose. Innovating enterprises have developed highly productive means of creating common purpose. They have broken through the internal barriers which divide parts of enterprises, including their leadership.

I believe that innovation and experimentation are risky issues from an employee's point of view, primarily because of the chance of failure and of censure, punishment or even dismissal. Companies claim that they want and need these attributes, but have not thought through the implications from the employees' perspectives.

At Telstra, Australia's government-owned and largest telecommunications provider, there are now approximately 50,000 employees, having been reduced from over 100,000, and the managing director has announced that this number must be reduced to approximately 30,000. If you are fearful that making mistakes will increase your chances of being made redundant, then being innovative and experimenting would be extremely risky in a Telstra-type environment. You would be much more likely to take these types of risk if you had the confidence in yourself that comes from pursuing your passion.

EMPLOYEE LOYALTY

Passionate employees create a conundrum: on the one hand, they are valuable, productive and effective, and are thus more attractive to their employer's competitors. On the other hand, if their passion is supported in the workplace, they will be aware that, even though competitors may offer more pay to entice them to move, being able to work in a supportive environment is difficult to achieve and so their willingness to move to a competitor will be reduced.

A number of my friends and clients have found themselves in this position as employees, and on many occasions, having taken the bait and left their existing employment for the higher income, very quickly regretted the move! The values that promoted their passion in the old workplace were not present in the new.

For employees, this underlines the importance of becoming aware of your values hierarchy, or scale of values, which I explored in Chapter 5: you can compare your hierarchy with that of your existing workplace and the new workplace. If you have spent the time and effort to become clear about your hierarchy of values, but the new employer does not have a firmly enunciated set of values, then you may be paying a large price in terms of your spirit for the increase in income. In addition, being clear about your values helps you assess the relative worth to you of the attractive pay offer: what price are you paying for the increased wealth?

Another benefit arises for employers: because most businesses have not invested the time and effort to enunciate the values within their business, those who have done so are able to educate their employees on the benefits *to them* of the employer's commitment to the values elicitation process. Employees who understand the benefits will be less likely to leave for a higher income.

PASSION AND TRUTH

I do not mean to repeat myself unnecessarily, but there are some concepts that I believe need to be repeated because they are different from what most of us have been taught. One such concept is the unique way that each human being sees and experiences life, the unique perspective that each one of us has. Most participants in my programs have acknowledged that, even though they *intellectually* know about this phenomenon, they still feel upset when others disagree with their opinions!

I, too (much to my chagrin) feel upset when someone disagrees with me, although the path that I have taken, and the lessons I have learned, in the last few years have at least increased my awareness about the source of my feelings and decreased their frequency. Where does the upset come from when someone disagrees with our opinion? It could be due to one or several of the following causes:

- the disagreement makes us feel that we are wrong
- the disagreement brings up our fears of inadequacy
- the disagreement might make us look foolish
- the disagreement might make others reject us
- the disagreement might lower other people's esteem of us.

The importance of the upset is to observe that it is there and that it emanates from our subconscious response to a perception of threat. I believe that the more we can accept others' views of the world without feeling threatened, the less fearful we will be and the more tolerant we will be. That tolerance leads us to be open to new ideas and new perspectives that can help us to advance in whatever direction we are hoping to go in.

My father, Zoltan (a fine Hungarian name! You might recognize it from *My Fair Lady*, when Eliza Doolittle attends her first socialite event; the Hungarian who is alleged to be competent to decide whether or not she is a fraud is 'Zoltan Karpathy'), analyzes this issue of being open to new ideas in a very simple way. He has often asked me:

What is the biggest hindrance to learning?

His answer?

"When the person you are talking to says "I know!""

The lesson he has taught me is a valuable one, that the block to learning is to have a closed mind. He has made me aware that everything that I hold dear can be challenged, and that if I close my mind to new perspectives or new pieces of information, I am reducing my capacity to learn. Indeed, Wayne Dyer, the well-known author, has written a book whose title says something similar: *You'll See It When You Believe It!* rather than the statement of many people that 'I'll believe it when I see it.' His point is that we usually see only what we are looking for, we see only what is consistent with our picture of how things are, so we can miss out on new ideas and concepts that may be too challenging to accept.

So, in your workplace, what happens when an employee tells the truth as he or she sees it? Do you, as an employee, tell the truth? If not, why not? What is the threat, or fear, if you tell the truth? If you are an employer, how do you respond to hearing the truth from an employee's perspective if it is not what you want to hear?

If your workplace encourages and supports you to follow your passion, you will have the self-confidence and the power to tell more truth than would otherwise be the case. I have worked with one of Australia's largest corporations, whose mission statement claims that its employees are one of its greatest strengths, and yet *every* employee of that corporation with whom I have spoken has laughed derisively when asked whether that statement is put into practice! Would you have the courage to point out this lack of congruence and integrity to the corporation's managing director if you were employed by it? If not, why not? Be aware of your response, because it contains valuable clues *for you* and what you believe about yourself. This is a dilemma in many companies: putting the *philosophy* of the value and importance of the employees into *practice*. As a well-known saying goes: 'It is easier to fight for your principles than it is to practice them!'

The Australian government's *Karpin Report*, to which I referred earlier, discovered that most Australian leaders and managers have inadequate people skills. This is no surprise; after all, where in our education system, either secondary or tertiary, are these skills taught? This lack of people skills is one of the reasons why I ceased to practice law, so that I could make a contribution in that field, and is one of the reasons why I am writing this book. While I was passionate about law, I am more passionate about passion itself, and I found that generating this passion in the workplace and in schools would require many significant changes.

The value to a business of hearing the truth is that the employer can make decisions based on fact, rather than fiction. Decision-making will therefore improve. The real issues that get in the way of innovation, continuous improvement, motivation, and productivity can then be addressed. My experience has been that many employees do not believe that their bosses want to hear the truth. To succeed in business, handling the truth is a necessity. Passionate employees will tell more truth than others!

PASSION AND GREAT TEAMWORK

From my 28 years of business experience, I believe it is clear that if employees are passionate, their ability and their willingness to create great teams is enormously enhanced, and the contribution that great teams make to any business is simply extraordinary. The challenge, as shown in hundreds of recently published management books, is to create great teams.

What is the key to teamwork? I have developed the following framework, which I use in my programs:

- The single most importance characteristic of a great team is excellent *communication* between team members.
- Excellent *communication* will occur between team members only when two elements are present:
  - *trust* between the team members; and
  - *commitment* to each other.
- Trust and commitment will flourish and grow only if team members are committed to a *common purpose*, common vision or common goal.
- Team members will commit to a common purpose if that purpose is congruent with their own purpose, congruent with their *personal goals*.

- Team members need to be clear on their personal goals, and the key to this clarity is that each team member know what he or she wants in life; in other words, the key is *self-knowledge*.

As you will realize by now, this book is all about self-knowledge, it is predicated on the basis that knowing ourselves is the key to our lives, and yet our system does not support us in this quest of self-knowledge.

The more that employees understand themselves and help to create a workplace that supports their passion, the easier it will be for the above steps towards great team-work to be taken and fulfilled. Please do not think that I am claiming that creating great teams is easy; I know it is not, but I do know that the results that great teams achieve are outstanding and worthwhile, and that not many organisations succeed in achieving them.

KEY POINTS FOR CHAPTER 6

- Review the subheads in this chapter.
- The more passionate you are, the greater your impact on other people.
- Passionate employees building better relationships create loyal customers.
- Passionate employees care for their customers: customers want to feel cared for!
- When you believe, you are believed! Belief increases your ability to sell anything.
- Passionate employees are more likely to tell the truth: this makes the business more able to handle the real issues that prevent outstanding results.

CHAPTER 7
Passionate Leaders & Managers

CHAPTER 7
Passionate Leaders & Managers

'*If we did all the things we are capable of doing, we would literally astound ourselves.*'

— Thomas A. Edison

Leadership and management are two different types of roles, and they are fulfilled by two different types of people. My simple, working distinction between the two is that the leader is a visionary and a motivator, while the manager helps the leader to achieve, or manage, the process of achieving the vision! However, the distinction between the two roles is frequently blurred, and most leaders often have to manage, and most managers often have to lead. I do not see the need in this book to explore the distinction to any greater extent than this. Suffice it to say, the importance of leaders and managers generally is unquestioned, and in the context of passion, is especially important.

Nothing is static in the universe, and maintaining the status quo in business is virtually impossible. Thus, there are really only two impacts that leaders and managers can have on the passion of their employees: they can either nurture it, or they can suppress it. Ignoring passion does not have a different impact, it will simply suppress it.

The first critical issue is the passion in the leader and the manager. If the leader is not passionate, it will be difficult to create an environment in which passion is nurtured. In these circumstances, the employees will have to generate the passion within themselves, or leave that organization. If you are a leader or manager but you are not passionate about your work, and you can see and want the difference that passion would make for your employees and for your business, all I can suggest is that you consider the ideas in Chapter 2 and do what you are intuitively attracted to do.

If you as a leader or manager have not been willing or courageous enough to do your own work of introspection, then you will not be able to encourage your employees to do so! Finding passion can be scary and risky and painful, but the rewards are far greater than the drawbacks. Make a decision that you want to find your passion, and as you progress along the path of inner wisdom and inner knowing, the path toward self-knowledge, your ability to bring your employees with you and to motivate them to access their own passion will increase in direct proportion.

Here are the key ways in which leaders and managers can nurture passion in their employees and in their workplace:

- Discover the highest possible purpose for your business.

- Discover what suppresses spirit and soul in your workplace and then do something about it.
- Demonstrate to the employees that the business is about more than making a profit.
- Engage the employees in the dream and the passion that started the business.
- Create an environment in which employees' hearts can be used, as well as their minds.
- Make employees *feel* they are important and do not just say it: this requires deeds as well as words.
- Find out what is important to the employees, what their dreams are, what they believe their lives are about.

Let's look at each of these in more detail.

DISCOVER THE HIGHEST POSSIBLE PURPOSE FOR YOUR BUSINESS

Your business has a higher purpose than just making a profit. The higher the purpose you can find, the more willing the employees will be to engage their minds as well as their hearts. If a business is just about making money, many people will refuse to engage all three aspects of their humanness, and simply do their job for their salary. The leader will be left yearning for more, and wondering why he or she 'cannot find good employees these days!'

Discover the higher purpose and spread the message to all of your employees. Share it with them and show that this higher purpose is important to the leaders and managers. Beware, however, of false messages: if the leaders do not believe in the higher purpose, it will not have the desired impact on the employees. Here are some questions that will help you to discover or remember the higher purpose of your business:

- Why was the business established?
- What contribution does the business make to its customers' lives?
- What value is the business adding?
- What contribution does the business make to our planet?
- Who benefits from the different activities of the business?
- What will be the benefits, other than financial gain, if the business achieves its goals?

A clearly articulated higher purpose has great power and attraction for employees as well as customers. There is a reason for employees to give their minds, bodies, and spirits to the purpose. To use a sporting analogy, the great achievements in team sport follow the creation of great spirit and camaraderie among the team members, and it is the higher purpose of the team's success that generates that team spirit. A renowned example of this was when the United States ice hockey team, in the 1984 Olympics, defeated the Russian team for the first time ever in the final and won the gold medal. This game was about more than ice hockey: the higher purpose was the battle between capitalism and communism, and the Americans were representing their whole nation. This higher purpose generated the momentum for the players to exceed their previous best.

When a leader can find and share a higher purpose, his or her ability to 'grab their hearts as well as their minds' will soar.

DISCOVER AND ELIMINATE
SUPPRESSORS OF SPIRIT AND SOUL

There are many ways in which the spirit of employees can be suppressed. Wide-eyed, excited youngsters (or even the more experienced veteran) arriving for work on their first day soon fall into the mould of putting up with the daily grind! How can this syndrome be avoided?

I explored many of these suppressors of spirit in Chapter 2, and I hope you will forgive me if I list them again. Consider this list and ask yourself which suppressors apply in your workplace. When you have consciously identified them, you can do something about them.

- Employees get no encouragement from their bosses.
- Employees get no recognition when they do a good job.
- Employees get no recognition when they put in a special effort.
- Employees have to do things that are contrary to the company's published values or to the employees' own values.
- Employees feel that they are treated like second-class citizens.
- Employees are given no credit for being able to think.
- Employees are not trusted and are not given responsibility.
- Employees are sometimes forced to tell lies to customers.

- Employees are 'put down' in front of others for making mistakes.
- Relationships between employees are strained and stressful.

DEMONSTRATE THAT THE BUSINESS IS ABOUT MORE THAN MAKING A PROFIT

This process is complementary to the process of discovering the higher purpose. The key word is to 'demonstrate,' as opposed to just making statements. A recurring theme in companies and organisations that I have worked with is the conflict between what is *said* to be important and the actual *behavior* of leaders. These conflicts have to be minimized to allow passion and spirit to flourish.

Living up to the values of the business is the key way to demonstrate this principle, and leaders should take the opportunity to show and tell the employees that the values are actually being observed. Repetition is important. Leaders and managers may think that the employees have been shown that values have been put into practice in the past, but all of us have so many contrary experiences that believing and trusting that the values will be practiced takes time.

The other challenge is one of different perspectives. You the leader may believe that the values of the company are being followed in practice, but your employees have a different perspective! They may have insufficient information, or they may close their minds to the facts, but it is their perspectives in this instance that need to be changed. The leader's job is to spend the time communicating and exploring these different perspectives, and to take the risk of being criticized, misinterpreted and misunderstood.

ENGAGE EMPLOYEES IN THE DREAM AND THE PASSION THAT STARTED THE BUSINESS

Every business is unique and has a unique history. Every business that exists on the planet today started as one human being's dream, which then became a thought or idea and, in the case of the great businesses, was driven by a passion. What is the dream and the passion that created the history of your business? When was the last time that the employees heard the history? Has the dream ever been shared with them?

There are approximately one million business enterprises in Australia, and each has a story, even the largest! BHP Co Ltd has a wonderful history, and the role that one man, Essington Lewis played in that history is very special. The culture that Lewis instilled is still having an impact today, some 70 years after his hands-on involvement. I have never worked with BHP, but what I have read and heard about Lewis has significantly changed my feelings towards the company for the better.

Another large Australian company I have worked with is Amcor Ltd, in its paper division. One of its key products with which most Australians are familiar is Reflex copy paper. I had the privilege of sharing and facilitating a weekend with senior managers at the company's Gippsland operations, which include forestry and nursery operations, paper production, and recycling. The vision of the company's employees 50 years ago is having an impact today in the extent of the pine and blue gum forests that the company owns.

I was inspired and impressed by hearing the story and understanding the courage of those long-dead employees: the experience certainly engaged my spirit and gave me a very positive perspective on both Amcor as a company and the benefit to the community of the continuing prosperity of such companies. Because Amcor processes trees for paper, it has been severely criticized by the environmental movement. What I and the others present learned showed the company's high level of commitment to sustainable forestry.

One of my smaller client companies is Gole Peden, a real estate company that started in the mid-1980's, powered by the dream and passion of Jeff Gole. I encouraged Jeff to share his dream and his passion with his employees, his sales consultants, and his clients, and the impact has been most beneficial. All those involved with the company can understand the bigger picture and put each activity into context, thus getting a *feel* for what they are each doing and the importance to the company's success of each person's individual contribution.

If you are a leader, and particularly if you are the founder of your business, share your dream and your vision and your passion with all of the company's employees; your chances of engaging their spirits and their passion will increase dramatically!

ENGAGE EMPLOYEES' HEARTS AS WELL AS THEIR MINDS

All human beings have feelings! This book is all about feelings. Our passion comes from our spirit, from our soul; it is a feeling, not a thinking process. However, most businesses seem to deny this fundamental human trait.

Does your business allow the existence and utilization of feelings? If not, you are reducing the opportunities for the existence of passion.

A number of processes are available to begin accessing feelings, and one that I use in most circumstances, because it is quick, simple and effective, is called a 'WIFL'—'What I Feel Like Saying.' I learned this valuable process in 1992 from the program 'Money and You.' Each of the teams in your business, whenever a formal meeting starts, can start with a WIFL, which requires each team member to access their *feelings*. Each team member speaks, without interruption, for an agreed period or for as long as that person *feels* the need, and expresses what the person *feels* like saying. This is not a *thinking* process, and through practice, team members become more comfortable with expressing their unique perspectives without feeling the need to censor, or suppress, their truth.

The commitment of the leader of the group to the process is the most important factor to ensuring that it is effective; if the leader does not fully and openly participate, the employees certainly will not do so. One of the key elements of the process is for others to listen actively without interruption, and this lack of interruption is most unusual today! Another key element is that there be no judgment of what team members say. There is no need to justify our feelings, and correspondingly there is no need for others to take on any blame for the feelings of another. This is easy to say and difficult to do, but the long-term benefits of regular WIFLs are proven.

WIFLs are also opportunities to express what we are actually feeling and to get into the practice of raising our awareness levels of those feelings. In Australia, our habit when we see each other is to say, 'Hello, how are you?' without any real desire to hear the response or to respond when we are asked. Even if we are willing to hear the response or to respond when it's our turn, the information given out is usually limited. Anthony Robbins, the famous motivational speaker, quoted some interesting statistics in one of his seminars which I attended. (By the way, if you get the chance to attend one of his programs, do not hesitate: they are wonderful.) Robbins says that most people use eight common words to describe how they are feeling, when the *Oxford English Dictionary* contains 3,000 different words to describe feelings!

Feelings are very subtle, and the differences between them can be difficult to find. To give participants in my programs an idea of the many possible ways to describe your feelings, I have prepared a list of over 500 different feelings: they are included in the Appendix. When you are stuck for words to describe your feelings, just scan the list! The more you look at, and learn from, the list, the more you will become aware of the extraordinary range of feelings that human beings are capable of feeling.

MAKE EMPLOYEES FEEL IMPORTANT

Employees can feel when they are important and valued. *Telling* them that this is the case will not *create* the feelings. If they do not feel it, they will not believe it!

Here are some of the deeds by which a leader can demonstrate that his or her employees are important and valuable:

- Commit to their ongoing learning and development and actually do something about it by organizing and investing in relevant programs.
- Understand that attending a training program will not cause radical changes in the employees overnight; a learning program is like a golf lesson: we learn the techniques, but for change to occur, ongoing repetition, practice, and mistakes are also required!
- Do what I suggest in the next section, and find out what is important to the employees.
- Give all employees clarity about what is expected of them in the workplace and how their performances will be assessed.
- Give employees the right to complain when the values of the business are not being observed.
- Commit to communicating with employees, and make allowances for their unique perspectives; this includes telling them when they've done something right as well as when they've done something wrong.
- Commit to a process of giving more trust to the employees. This process, by definition, cannot be

achieved overnight, but until the leader demonstrates trust, the employees will not be willing to trust. Trust needs to built like a brick wall, brick by brick, day by day, and there needs to be a high awareness of how easily and quickly the brick wall can be demolished.

Here is a practical example of how trust can be won and lost in the work environment. A close friend of mine, who shall remain nameless, was working for one of Australia's largest publicly listed resource companies. He was a mid-level manager who was not afraid to express his views. I visited him to explore how we could benefit each other, and he told me about the training that had been done within the organization for the last two years with the aim of raising the level of leadership skills of middle managers and increasing the levels of trust and open communication. He told me that the company recognized the need for repetition over a period of time to build trust.

Some months later, he called me to say he'd been sacked, along with 35 percent of all mid-level managers, because the company had been criticized in the press for low profit levels and the managing director had decided that something needed to be done immediately! These middle managers were sacked contrary to the philosophy and the commitments that had been pursued and practiced over the previous two years.

My friend also told me that the remaining employees had immediately withdrawn their trust and their communication. So two years of work and effort was wasted! In addition, the managing director was quoted in a full-page interview in the Australian business press as saying how important the employees were to the future of the company.

I took a particular interest in the performance of this company over the next 12 months and noted that its results had not improved, creating considerable pressure on the executives to improve the situation drastically. I believe that trust within the company had been significantly damaged, and it continued to be low because the words did not match the deeds. Subsequently, the managing director was retrenched.

How could passion of employees flourish in such an environment?

On the other hand, there are some wonderful examples of leaders who do care for their employees, and make them feel important. In my opinion, Alan Scott, a great Australian businessman and leader, is one such person. I interviewed Alan because I admired his company's achievements and had the fortune to meet him socially. He agreed to allow me to tell the story of his success.

Alan graduated in mechanical engineering from a university in 1952. On Labour Day in 1960, he joined Gerry Lincolne, whose father had started Lincolne & Co in 1910. The company increased in size to eight people, but the war decimated the engineering profession. When Alan started with Gerry, there were four staff, and Alan's financial interest in the firm was a mere 2.5 percent. Now in 2002, there are 450 staff in 15 offices around Australia and Asia. He started in business with a philosophy, a culture, and a morality, and said to himself, 'Let's see what happens!' There was no specific vision. There was no specific target.

Alan Scott's philosophy was to reproduce himself: he thought at the time that this was the obvious thing to do! He did not want to be a 'hands-on' engineer: he wanted others to be developed so that they were able to do the work; he would then be able to do the really hard and challenging work of thinking and planning. Accordingly, he adopted as one of his keys to success: 'Always employ someone who is better than you are.' Within Lincolne Scott, there were no 'poor cousin' sections: all employees were treated well, and all were considered to be important to the group's long-term success.

Another of his keys to success, which supported this commitment to the employees, was 'to be so good at what you do that people come to you.' Clients were so impressed with the service that they became the best marketing arm of the business!

Alan believes that society and the universe reward you based upon your contribution. He had no specific vision for the future other than wanting to offer others the opportunities he had enjoyed. If he knew how to reproduce himself, then he could delegate work successfully and the client would not suffer as a consequence. He used the Prime Minister's salary as his touchstone for his success. If he could earn what the Prime Minister was earning, then he could consider that he was successful.

He describes himself as an idealist, someone with an ideal who pursues it. 'I was determined to meet clients' needs,' he said. Alan felt excited right from the start of his career about his desire to create a tangible and living entity through the business. Reproducing himself was the greatest excitement because he could see no limits to the process. He considered that he had obligations to all of his family, other people, his employees, his religion, and society in general to give the best of himself.

Determination has also been a key factor in his successful life. Alan believes that 'if you do the right thing for the right price, then you will make money.' He also had a commitment to protect the families of those who worked for him. I asked him what he loved. The answer: 'The intellectual challenges to meet needs and wants by the use of my skills through the construction industry.'

Soul is also important to Alan. He has an ideal of service, and this ideal has played a long-term, important role in his family. He believes he is a trustee of people's health, money, and well being. Religion also plays a significant part in his life.

What does he hate? 'I hate losing.' Hating to lose is different to being afraid of losing, but he only wanted to win if his self-respect was preserved, if he was able to act with integrity. He believes that there are certain aspects of morality to competing, and that one of the complexities within business relationships is that everyone has his or her own rules of morality.

Did he have much fun? He has always enjoyed challenges, and that enjoyment enabled him to be keen on what he was doing through almost all of his long business career.

He has been able to enjoy his work, and almost always felt a state of excitement, a sense of urgency. 'Tomorrow's too late because there'll be more to do tomorrow.'

Would he ever describe himself as passionate? 'Not in work. I do not like to use extreme words. I would describe others such as: Australia's former Prime Minister Paul Keating as passionate.' Alan sees a lack of philosophical integrity in our politicians because of the politics of hate, and the process that requires constant attacks of other people rather than the points of view held by those people.

Leadership is about generating a workable result for the people you are serving: 'I get more pleasure from giving than from receiving.' Alan always felt that he wanted to prevent oppression, 'and giving opportunities is the opposite of oppression.' He hated oppression: it drove him into creating and giving opportunities to many people! Alan wants his people to grow. In his view, oppressive managers are bad managers.

He runs the business on a paternalistic basis, considering himself to be like a father to the employees. Recently, it took him two years to eradicate a culture of cynicism which had crept into the business. He was patient and determined in the eradication process: he knew it would take time, that there was no quick and easy solution.

I asked him finally which books had made a big impact on him. Alan said that Douglas McGregor's book, **The Human Side of Enterprise,** was the one book in particular that had had a great influence on his success.

ACKNOWLEDGE WHAT IS IMPORTANT TO THE EMPLOYEES

What are your employees' dreams, what do they want? If an employee's needs and wants are fulfilled within the workplace, passion can thrive and flourish. Discovering the needs and wants is not easy, and this book demonstrates why this is so. Nevertheless, making a commitment to fulfill these needs and wants will have a significant positive impact on employees.

One easy way to begin this process is to invest in learning and development programs whose outcomes include the gaining of increased clarity by employees about their lives and their wants, their needs, their goals.

There are plenty of ideas throughout this book on how to find out what the employees want: all the leader has to do is to commit to the process, and this commitment will happen if the leader accepts the benefits that are likely to flow in terms of the sustainable success of the business.

I do not propose to explore the key ways in which leaders and managers can suppress passion in their employees and their workplace: I know that is happening with monotonous regularity in most workplaces without the need for more ideas. If leaders concentrate on the positives, the negative influences will not have the opportunity to dominate as they presently do.

A final thought: I was searching the Internet recently and wandered onto the Harvard Business School website. Here I found the synopsis of an article in the March 1997 edition of the Harvard Business Review entitled 'The Living Company.' The author, Arie de Geus, a retired Shell executive, seeks to explain the longevity gap between centuries-old companies and the average corporation, which does not last five years.

The conclusion is that the managers of 'living companies' that last for many years have a number of things in common. They all:

- consider themselves to be stewards of a long-standing enterprise
- are like careful gardeners; they encourage growth and renewal without endangering the plant they are tending
- value profits the same way most people value oxygen: as necessary for life but not the purpose of it
- are willing to make dramatic changes to ensure survival
- constantly search for new ideas
- focus on developing people; they create opportunities for employees to learn from one another.

I take comfort from these conclusions of de Geus, which reinforce for me the reasons for writing this book.

KEY POINTS FOR CHAPTER 7

- Review the subheads in this chapter.
- Leaders and managers are different but complementary.
- Leaders must be passionate if they want passionate employees.
- Remember the dream that started every business: inspiration is a *soul* exercise, not a *mind* exercise.
- Passionate leaders create a powerful metaphysical attraction in others.
- Allow space in the business for feelings.
- When leaders give trust and open communication, they will receive trust and open communication in return.
- Leaders who care for their employees will create outstanding results.

CHAPTER 8
How to Protect or Encourage Passion in Your Child

CHAPTER 8
How to Protect or Encourage Passion in Your Child

'Life is either daring adventure, or nothing. Security does not exist in nature, nor do the children of men as a whole experience it. Avoiding danger is no safer in the long run than exposure.'

— Helen Keller

*T*he education system in the Western world, and in Australia in particular, does not encourage us, or teach us, to find our passion!

The schools I attended, those that my family attended and those that my four children presently attend all pay little attention to individual passion. There is simply no structured process or system to help students in this process.

The assumption seems to be that students will know what their passion is, and the job of the school is simply to educate so that the student can be gainfully and successfully employed in the future. For those students who do not know what they're passionate about, the message is to keep studying, get the best results that you can, and eventually you'll find your passion.

I do not believe that this process works, and my view is that leaving the discovery of our children's passion to the education system is highly unlikely to be successful. I do not mean to criticize teachers: they are simply repeating the patterns of the past.

As we have seen so far in this book, there are various structured ways and strategies for finding our passion, and these ways can be taught. Schools can change their attitudes, and *will* change if parents are supportive of such changes. Parents who read this book can begin to encourage the schools that their children attend to implement processes set out in this book. Guest speakers or other outsiders can be brought in if teachers feel they are unqualified to make these changes.

Daily newspapers continue to spread one of the key challenges of the twenty-first century: from where are the jobs coming? Where has our security gone? Parents see a 'dog-eat-dog' employment market, where the only young people who will get jobs are those who achieve extraordinary results in their final year of school, thus leading to the situation where allegedly desirable professions, such as law, medicine, and dentistry, now set prohibitively high 'scores' for entrance to the relevant university courses.

This strategy is, in my view, doomed to failure. There are no safe or secure jobs being created, and none that can be created. Governments are simply unable to 'create' in this way! We now live in the technological age, the knowledge age, where the rate of change is probably faster than any other time in history.

Unless our children pursue their passion, they will

remain in a state of struggle! The only work available will be the opportunities that they themselves create.

FULLER'S VIEWS ON JOBS

I am aware that I have referred to Buckminster Fuller on numerous occasions in this book. I have to admit that he is one of my heroes, one of the people whose views and opinions I respect and, indeed, follow and use as guidelines in my daily work.

I was first exposed to his work in detail in November 1992, when I attended the program 'Money and You.' A few months later, in June 1993, I met his assistant Amy Edmondson, who has written of her three years' work with Fuller in *A Fuller Explanation*, subtitled *The Synergetic Geometry of R. Buckminster Fuller.* In her book, Edmondson explains for a lay audience the concepts behind Fuller's life work.

Fuller's life and his achievements were extraordinary. Over the course of his life, he was conferred 47 honorary degrees from various universities around the world! For that reason it is even more extraordinary that his work and discoveries are not generally taught to our children.

Let me quote from the dust jacket of *Bucky Works*, written in 1996 by J. Baldwin, an inventor and teacher who worked under, with and for Fuller for more than three decades:

> Architect, mathematician, engineer, inventor, visionary humanist, educator, inspirational orator, and best-selling author, R. Buckminster Fuller has been rightly called "the twentieth century Leonardo

Da Vinci." Over the course of his long life, Fuller was showered with official honours for his contributions to design science as well as his pioneering work in the 'whole systems' approach to solving global problems. But he is probably best remembered for his futuristic inventions—most notably, the geodesic dome, the strongest, most cost-effective structure ever devised. Since his death in 1983, appreciation for Fuller's ideas has grown steadily worldwide, culminating in 1995—the year of his centenary—with an unprecedented series of tributes and commemorative events…

"Bucky Works: Buckminster Fuller's Ideas for Today" is a celebration of the man and his ideas. More than just a biographical account or a historical treatise, it is a thought-provoking consideration of the importance of the Fuller legacy to our future and an inspiring synthesis of Fuller's major ideas and inventions.

Just to complete the picture of this man, I have been told that he had the longest entry of any person in *Who's Who* in the United States!

Fuller's views on jobs are valuable and instructive. Chapter 11 of *Bucky Works* is devoted to the topic 'Jobs and Work.' I do not wish to quote extensively from it: rather, I'll attempt to paraphrase in point form Baldwin's explanation of Fuller's key messages:

- Working for an illusory security turns human beings into robots, or automatons.
- Human beings were not designed to work for

financial security, with a health plan, and the
prospect of a pleasant retirement.

- The urge towards financial security leads to
  psychological fortress-building, and a defensive
  state of mind rather than a creative state.
- Real security comes from using our imagination,
  taking risks, and having adventures: in this way,
  we move too fast, and we are too agile, to be hit
  by the vast array of speedy changes that assault
  us today and will continue so to do.
- While there are risks in this type of philosophy
  and practice, there are just as many, albeit different
  ones, in seeking financial security.
- There are fewer jobs as a consequence of technological advance, and the number will continue to
  reduce; as a simple example, witness the reduction
  of bank tellers with the proliferation of automatic
  teller machines.
- Lifetime careers are gone forever.
- Real security comes from each one of us pursuing
  our own 'personal projects,' the opportunities that
  each one of us sees where we can solve problems,
  or 'add value.'
- Avoid specializing too much. Bucky described
  himself as a 'generalist,' and he noted that generalists
  were more flexible and adaptable than specialists.
- Nature rewards generalists and eliminates specialists.
- Teaching and learning are what we are here on this
  planet Earth to do. Seeking to be secure limits our
  learning and our ability to teach.

SPECIFIC STRATEGIES FOR YOUR CHILDREN AT HOME

I believe that human beings are born possessing a great range of intuitive skills. Anyone who is a parent knows that a three-year-old child:

- knows what she wants
- can clearly express what she wants
- can manipulate her parents
- can negotiate with her parents, or, indeed, any other humans.

It has also been my experience, speaking generally, that most 18-year-old school dropouts seem to have lost these intuitive skills; they seem to have been educated in favor of the data learning that dominates our Western-style education systems.

I have interviewed many graduates of universities and tertiary institutions, particularly of law schools, and these graduates were some of the highest-scoring 'products' of the Australian education system. The skill level of these graduates in terms of intuitive skills was exceedingly disappointing! Very few of them knew what they wanted, other than to 'get a job' as a lawyer. Very few had confidence in themselves, or at least showed confidence during in the interview process. Very few understood basic business issues in Australia, having specialized to such an extent during their school and university days that they did not have time to read the business section of newspapers or magazines.

There are specific ways to address this waste of intuition, this waste of intuitive and natural skill. My suggestions are:

- Encourage mistakes and a love of learning.
- Look for the 'clues.'
- Encourage meditation.
- Encourage intuitive skills.
- Keep a journal.
- Practice communication, both with your children and their friends… particularly listening skills.
- Minimize the criticism.
- Demonstrate that you are 'living your passion' or, if not, that you wish you had done so!
- Accept responsibility for the education of your children.
- Practice balancing mind/body/spirit in the home.

I will deal with each of these strategies separately.

ENCOURAGE MISTAKES AND A LOVE OF LEARNING

I have written at length about the value of mistakes, and the price that we pay, as human beings, if we continue to punish those who make mistakes. There is no doubt in my mind that putting this concept into practice is difficult: I have been working on it for some years now, and still find that I cannot avoid being upset with myself, let alone others, when certain types of mistakes are made.

Nevertheless, the fact that it is hard does not mean that it cannot be done! Everything that I have learned has shown me that all great achievers in life have made lots of mistakes; in fact, they make more mistakes than most people. A person who makes no mistakes achieves nothing of worth. It is our years of education and training that have taught us that mistakes will lead to pain of some sort, be it physical or mental punishment, lower marks, loss of money or job, demotion, and so on. That is why we seem to want to protect our children from making mistakes, and why we punish them when they make them.

But they have to make them! If you protect them when they are young, they will make the mistakes when they are older. The older they are, the higher the price of the mistake. Thus, there is a lifelong benefit in making as many mistakes as we can as quickly as possible, so that we *learn* what life is about sooner rather than later! If you punish your children for their mistakes, they will avoid making them. Their capacity to learn will be diminished, along with their ability to learn quickly.

I suggest a specific alternative strategy: adopt the philosophy within your family that 'Mistakes are wonderful learning experiences,' or that 'Mistakes are good,' or whatever words sit comfortably with you. Put the words on a poster, display it in your home, and teach your children that you want to practice this philosophy, that if you abuse them or punish them for making mistakes, then they should point out your failure to follow the philosophy. Remember: this could be difficult and challenging, and you will need to practice! Remember also, that practice does not make perfect, rather, that 'Practice makes Better'!

Of course, there are different types of mistakes, and it can be helpful to clarify your position and your thinking and beliefs on the matter. When I use the term 'mistakes,' I mean an action that is taken in good faith, or an attempt made in good faith, that has led to an error. Examples for young children are:

- falling over when learning to walk
- falling off a bike when learning to ride
- incorrectly transcribing a telephone number
- dropping a glass and breaking it
- losing a library book.

Imagine abusing a young child for falling off a bike! And yet, that is what we do, time and time again. A far more helpful response is to give encouragement to try, try again.

A different category of mistakes would encompass, using the above examples:

- deliberately transcribing the telephone number incorrectly in order to aggravate a parent
- deliberately dropping the glass
- deliberately 'losing' the library book.

In these circumstances, the specific incorrect action is not a mistake: there was no attempt to achieve a goal. And yet, at a deeper level, there has indeed been a mistake: in the three examples above, the child has deliberately done something with an ulterior purpose, such as gaining attention, or exacting revenge, or causing embarrassment to the parent. At this deeper level, the apparent mistake was that aggravating the parent would lead to the child getting what the child wants.

Children are intuitively and naturally inquisitive and curious. When you punish them for making mistakes, you punish them for practicing new skills, new strategies and new attitudes. You are unconsciously squashing their spirit, their soul, their nature! Each time we squash a child's spirit, we make it more difficult for the child to access his or her unique passion, his or her unique essence. An ever-increasing love of learning is what results from ceasing to punish mistakes!

Learning is difficult and scary and stress-creating because of our fear of making mistakes, or our fear of the consequences of making mistakes. Recall now your own learning experiences throughout your childhood, and decide how they have influenced your present attitude to learning new skills. What is your attitude when you need to learn a new skill at work or at home? Are you aware that your tension level has increased? Has your heart rate changed? Can you feel yourself blushing? The more you become aware of your responses at these times, the more you can learn about the origins of these feelings. Ask yourself: if I were not facing fears, how would I be feeling? Because we live in such changing times, where few of us can predict what is going to be useful to know in the future, a love of learning can help to keep us on the learning path, to be willing to develop our skills, to be willing to make mistakes, to continue to learn by trial and error. Our children will need to learn on the job: their willingness to do so, and thus their rate of progress in any organization, will be greatly influenced by their love, or hate, or something in between, of the learning process and experience.

Sometime ago I received a postcard from a good friend, inviting me to a fourth anniversary reunion of our Hawaiian Business School graduates. The card said: 'What we learn with pleasure, we never forget.' I heartily endorse this statement, because it is consistent with my own experience. Another way of saying the same thing is that when we learn with emotion, the learning is deeper and more lasting. This appears to be true whether the emotion is pleasure or pain! The problem is that, if we learn in a painful way, as many people in our education system do, then we will want to avoid the learning environment and the learning opportunities. This will make us less adaptable, more fearful, and less able to be the successful human beings we were designed to be.

Learning can be fun, and parents can create such a fun environment in their homes. The more this is created, the weaker the potential influence of outside learning experiences, particularly school life. A wonderful book that explores these fun ways of learning, both at home and at school, is Bobbi De Porter's *Quantum Learning*. These different learning strategies or styles have been developed from the science of Neurolinguistic Programming, and the concept of accelerated learning, based on the leading-edge work done in the 1970s by a Bulgarian educator, Georgi Lozanov.

LOOK FOR THE 'CLUES'

When you, as a parent, decide that accessing passion is a worthwhile endeavor, then you will be motivated to become more aware of the 'clues' that your children give you from time to time about themselves. These clues can be very subtle. They include:

- activities that create excitement and spontaneous arousal
- activities that your children resist less than others
- activities that children persist in requesting.

The behavior of children is much more spontaneous than that of adults, and accordingly the *natural* inclinations of the children are what you seek to identify. These are not *learned* behaviors, they are not thinking behaviors; they are behaviors to which the child's soul is attracted. The more you become aware of these behaviors, the more you learn about your child's soul. Record these clues (in a journal, which I will mention below).

ENCOURAGE MEDITATION

This book does not teach meditation strategies, but I believe that every human being can benefit from practicing the art of meditation. It is the starting point for 'getting in touch with our selves.' How can we 'know ourselves' if we do not spend any time in solitude, in silence, listening to our quiet inner voice?

Meditation is beneficial whenever it is done, regardless of the time spent, but there is no doubt that practice makes better! The more I meditate, the greater the benefits I experience. Like many skills, the earlier we begin to learn them, the easier it is to learn, and so creating the opportunities for our children to learn to meditate will give them a valuable gift and resource for the rest of their lives, regardless of what their passion may be.

Your children will learn the value of getting in touch with themselves, of accessing their feelings, of becoming aware of their feelings and their individual, and unique, inner voice. As parents, giving permission to children to access these aspects of their humanness will have a direct and beneficial result.

While flying back from Hong Kong in May 1997, I read an article in *Newsweek* magazine on the issue of youth suicide. The article subhead read: 'Young men are killing themselves in record numbers, and a society that prizes rugged individualism is groping for ways to reach out to those at risk.'

The article discussed the life and recent suicide of a young professional rugby league footballer, David Woods. Youth suicide, and particularly by young men, is very much an issue in Australia, and I believe that the messages in this book are relevant to the prevention of suicide. The conclusion of the article's author, Melissa Roberts, is that young men, and young people generally, need to be able to communicate what they feel, and that Australian society does not encourage the necessary 'introspection' that enables or allows this to occur. David Woods' brother is quoted as having said: 'Boys can't communicate what they feel. They are socialised to be hard, tough, independent men who do not show their feelings. We need to tell them: "You are worthwhile. Seek help." Research suggests that more young girls attempt suicide, but more boys are successful, because they use more violent methods.

I agree with the conclusion in the article. It is my view that meditation of any type is a fundamental skill that will facilitate this introspection process.

ENCOURAGE INTUITIVE SKILLS

One of the possible team agreements that I encourage business teams to consider adopting is 'In cases of doubt, we agree to trust and rely upon our intuition.'

Our intuition and our intuitive skills are valuable and precious, and if they are not nurtured and encouraged, can be forgotten. Exercising these skills is the only way to develop them. It is like a golf or tennis swing: if not practiced, these are easily forgotten! I believe that using these skills increases our ability to find our passion, and to survive and prosper in changing times. Great businesses rely on accessing these skills, and I will deal with this in the following chapter. Children who are allowed to rely on these skills from an early age will learn to trust them and use them. I cannot put the value of trusting in our own intuition any better than Ken Carey has done in **Return of the Bird Tribes:**

You are all God beings *in potential* with no reason not to become God beings in reality. Trust yourself, trust your natural response to each new situation. The action arising from within your heart is not going to be destructive, it is going to suggest the most creative path to walk in answer to your situation and your world. When you trust yourself, you are trusting in the Wisdom that designed you. This is how you trust in God. It is not an abstract thing.

Trust in God is trusting in the God who lives within you, trusting in your spirit's ability to respond to each situation beautifully, impeccably, individually, creatively. When you doubt your native ability to breathe the air of spirit into your world and create according to your divine thought, you are doubting both God and the universe. You are rejecting life's most precious gift to you—your own inner knowing—and you are presuming to replace it with values, judgments and opinions you have acquired second hand…

There is a movement of spirit that proceeds from within your heart to greet the world with the clarity of perfect action. That movement is intuitive. It is your direct link with the Source of all life. In the instant you know what to do, and in the same instant, you flow into the perfect action required. Trust your intuition. It is an arrow whose shaft has been carved straight and smooth; unerring and true it flies to its mark. Can the ponderous tread of the rational mind be compared to the swift, sure flight of an arrow? Reason is designed to support, not to lead your action. It is meant to help you implement the purposes of your heart; it is not meant to determine them.

When I first read this passage, and every time I have done so since, my inspiration has increased, my trust in myself has strengthened, and my resolve to keep practicing my intuitive skills is renewed.

PRACTICE COMMUNICATION

How will you ever be good at communicating with your children if you do not practice? Are you a good communicator? Where did you learn to communicate? Ask your spouse or your family, and listen with humility to the answer.

I am the father of four children, ages 20, 18, 15, and 15 (the latter two are twins). There is no doubt that my ongoing communication level with them is enhanced by repetition and practice. When I lose myself in my work, or in writing, I lose contact with them. While they respect my need for solitude, they also 'clam up,' and it takes time to reestablish the level of good communication that I desire.

You are the leader of your children. If you do not communicate your true feelings, then they won't communicate back to you; and if you believe that your children are unable to tell if you are faking the truth, please think again. Remember, their innate intuitive skills enable them to 'smell a rat,' and they will intuitively know if you are being open or closed. The more open you are with them, the more open they will be with you!

I acknowledge the problems associated with being fully open, and I am not suggesting that *everything* is relevant to the children. However, protecting our children from our parental concerns and issues treats them like second-class people whose opinions are not valuable, and so they do not feel trusted. If they do not feel your trust, why would they give you their trust?

Listening is often a challenge for parents, including me. Nevertheless, I have learned, and I am continuing to learn, the meaning of quality listening, of active listening, without judgment, without comment, without interruption. Each of our children is unique, with a unique perspective, and each time that we criticize or judge their views, even with the best of intent, we squash their spirit, their individuality, their passion. Quality listening gives children an opportunity to express themselves *safely*, to speak their truth as they see and feel it. The safer they feel to tell the truth, the more you as a parent will hear.

The other benefit that comes from allowing children to express themselves is that the actual process of expression, of getting the words out, has a more lasting impact on the speaker than simply thinking a thought. Therefore, each time the child speaks about feelings, about dreams, about inspiration, about intuition, he or she is practicing what I would describe as a crystallization process, and the child's ability in the future to access the memory, to remember the inspiration, is strengthened.

It is easy to think of practical examples of this process. Imagine yourself as a young child, 'day-dreaming' about emulating Madonna, the world-famous singer, whose videos and deliberately outrageous behaviors have impressed you. Imagine your father, who may be a university professor, asking you what you are thinking about and you tell him. He explodes in anger! He upsets you, and criticises you. Then, years later, when you have forgotten what you were passionate about, and you are attending a personal development program, you are encouraged to remember what you used to 'daydream' about: your ability to recall the Madonna daydreaming episode will be significantly greater in this example than if you had avoided answering your father's questioning and therefore not 'crystallized' your thinking. The expression of your thoughts in words gives greater momentum to the instantaneous, intuitive discovery.

An alternative example could encompass the father responding positively to your daydream, and giving you such validation, such positive and confidence-building feelings, that the memory years later will be able to be accessed more readily than would have been the case if the day-dream had not been expressed in words. A short way to reinforce this example, and to remember it, is:

Everything begins with a thought.

Then, there is the word.

Then, there is the deed.

Then, there is an outcome.

Your children are not the only possible communication links: their friends are also valuable sources. If you take the time to listen to the views, hopes and aspirations of these friends, you gain a new and broader perspective of what might be happening with your own children. The friends will often be more open with you than with their own parents, and they can also share with you the special insights that they may have gained about your children. Because each human being is unique, each perspective is unique, and the insights and observations that the friends have about your children, if you take the time to listen, will assist you to help your children know themselves better.

MINIMIZE THE CRITICISM

How do you feel when you are criticized? Check inside yourself now, and remember those feelings. In an earlier chapter of this book, I have explored the damage that negative criticism can cause in the work environment with adults; I believe that criticism of children is even more destructive.

Each time we criticize our children, we squash their spirit, their intuitive nature. As parents, our psychological impact on our children is great, so the words with which we criticize have great power and a long-lasting impact. Remember that learning with emotion is a very powerful learning, and so, for children, being criticized and being told that they are no good or not clever enough or not quick enough, by their parents is well learned indeed. Constant and repetitious criticism by a parent will ensure that the child's trust in self, and reliance on intuition, is reduced and the child's ability to access and follow passion is retarded.

As Buckminster Fuller has said, we attempt to mold the behavior of children through the learning and criticism process to protect them from the pain and humiliation of mistakes, but in that process we deny them a critically important asset: their own inner knowing, their intuitive, God-given skills. Why should children think like their parents, dress like their parents, behave like their parents? If parents truly accept that each of their children is unique, there is a price to pay, and that price is to allow that uniqueness to flourish without treating differences in behavior, in thought, or in beliefs as a rejection of the parents. I have seen many instances of parents attempting to blackmail their children into certain behaviors and beliefs by threatening the withdrawal of their love; or the comment is made that 'if you behave in that way, it proves that you do not love me.'

I encourage you to think and feel about this issue, and if you are aware that criticism is a teaching or motivational strategy that you use as a parent, observe the impact that it has had to date, both on you and on your children.

DEMONSTRATE THAT YOU ARE 'LIVING YOUR PASSION'

Parents are a constant source of inspiration, either negative or positive, for their children. What we are, and do, as parents has, I believe, a far greater impact upon our children than what we tell them to do; in other words, our children are more likely to emulate our behaviors than heed our advice to them, if there is a discrepancy between the two. Many research studies have explored this phenomenon, but I do not wish to quote sources to you. Observe your own experience, and the experiences of parents around you to verify the finding.

If you are living your passion, this will have had, and will continue to have, a profound effect on your children and on those with whom both you and they relate. Earlier in the book I shared the anecdotal evidence I have collected which suggests that less than 10 percent of people in the workplace impress others as being passionate. If your children are fortunate enough to have one or more parents in this minority category, they already have a head start; I have no doubt that my children are in this minority. I demonstrate that I love what I do, that I am following my passion, and my children therefore receive constant reinforcement in thought, word and deed that discovering and following passion is one of the keys to a successful life.

I have also shared with them the process I went through to change from practicing law to establishing a successful business in a new, apparently unrelated field of education. They have often expressed the wish that my income had not shrunk for a while after the transition, but each time they did so, I explained why I took the risks, and the benefits to both them and me of following my passion.

What if you are not following your passion? First of all, take the steps set out in this book to increase your awareness of why you are not doing so, and what gets in the way of doing so. The clarity that you gain about yourself will benefit you, as well as increase your ability to explain your process to your children so that their awareness increases. Teaching in this way is real education, is useable, practical, impressive education!

The more willing you are to face your own truth, and to share that with your children, the greater the opportunity for them to become inspired to follow their own passion.

ACCEPT RESPONSIBILITY FOR THE EDUCATION OF YOUR CHILDREN

Do you leave the education of your children to their schools? While you may be paying a lot of hard-earned money to the schools, I believe that only 30 percent of children's education comes from school, regardless of how good the school is; 70 percent comes from you and the other influences on their lives. After all, in any year of the 12 years of formal schooling, a child spends only about 6 hours in class per day, for 40 weeks—a total of 1,200 hours. This is only 13 per cent of the child's life of 8,736 hours per year, and only 24 percent of the 5,840 hours per year that the child is awake, assuming 8 hours' sleep per night!

The skills you use today to generate your income were not learned predominantly at school, and your awareness and acceptance of this fact can galvanize you into sharing your hard-won 'living' skills with your children. Are you even aware of the range and depth of skills that you now have, that you have developed through the pain and the pleasure of your life to date? Which of these do you wish your children could have? While we all have to learn our lessons, there can be more or less efficient ways of learning them.

To assist you in your awareness, here is a list of some of the skills that you have probably developed and which you use in your personal and work lives:

- communication skills
- conflict-resolution skills
- negotiation-skills
- rapport-building skills
- speed-reading skills
- time-management skills
- information-research skills
- selling-skills
- marketing-skills.

This list could be much longer, but it is intended as a trigger to make you realize just how much you have learned to date, and to give yourself conscious credit for having done so! Then, when you appreciate yourself, and you are grateful for what you have learned, you may be motivated to spend time with your children to impart that knowledge. The knowledge can be imparted in a fun, time-effective way. Here is one example of how I do it in the context of teaching marketing skills to my children.

I use McDonald's Corporation as my model: after all, every child knows the business! I then ask my children to think about, and to explain in their own words, why McDonald's does what it does in any area of its business. Take, for example, marketing. I ask them to think about the advertisements for the hamburgers, the 'giveaways,' the incentives, the calendars, the concept of Ronald McDonald House. Their attempts to answer these questions have given them valuable insights into the marketing process, and to increase their awareness of how companies market their products to the younger generation.

PRACTICE BALANCING MIND, BODY, AND SPIRIT IN THE HOME

What proportions of your life do you contribute to your mind, body, and spirit aspects? Do you believe that they need to be in balance? Or do you face your life and wish that you could have some balance, but that earning your living takes too much time? The answer to this question depends on how you live your values, as dealt with in Chapter 5.

Accessing and demonstrating passion involves your spirit, your soul: if you do not give time to your spirit in the home, then your children do not experience, do not feel that side of you. They learn that mind and body take priority, so they will emulate you.

How do you access your spirit and give it time? As I have stated above, do the things that I have suggested in this book, or other steps that appeal to you or come into your awareness as being attractive to you as a consequence of being provoked by something that you have read here. If you search, you will find what you need, but if you do not search, then you will continue to generate the results that you have experienced to date, and your children will be likely to follow you. If you start and continue the search, your children will notice, and you will have an impact upon them that makes it okay for them to give more time to their spirit.

'Of the spirit' or 'spiritual' can include religious practice and observation, although that is not my predominant focus. I practiced Christianity (Catholicism) reasonably strictly for the first 40 years of my life, particularly by attending Mass in accordance with the rules of the Church. Since that time I have lost the desire or the need to practice religion. My children all attend Catholic schools, but I have chosen to let them make up their own minds on the level of observation of the Church's 'rules.' A major benefit of attending such schools is that there are many references made to God, spirit, and Christ throughout the school year, which serves to raise their awareness of spiritual, or at least, metaphysical matters.

KEEP A JOURNAL

Keep the observations from all of the above strategies in a journal or a diary. Our memories may not be as good as we think. In my life, particularly in matters of insight and intuition, I have had brilliant ideas and thoughts that I did not write down, and I have been unable to recall them again! Ever!

When you notice a clue, or you have an insight, *write it down!* Your children will thank you, and your ability to lead them toward their destiny will be enhanced to significant degree.

KEY POINTS FOR CHAPTER 8

- Review the subheads in this chapter.
- Future 'jobs' for your children will need to be created by themselves.
- Passion gives you internal security so that you have less need for external security.
- Children who follow their passion will be more able to add value to others' lives.
- You are more important than schools for the education of your children.
- More introspection may help to reduce youth suicide
- Daydreaming is valuable because it helps children to access their passion.
- Your children will communicate if you communicate first.
- Your childen need business skills that are not taught in school: you can remedy this!

CHAPTER 9
Specific Strategies
for Your Child
at School

CHAPTER 9

Specific Strategies for Your Child at School

'What we learn with pleasure,
we never forget.'

— **Author unknown**

*Y*ou are not at school with your child, so that any strategies for change need to be adopted by your child's school. My hope is that, after reading this book, you will encourage the school to think about the benefits of adopting the necessary and desirable changes that are set out below. My suggestions for parents are:

- Understand the philosophy behind the school's mission statement.
- Understand what the school presently does to develop the unique attributes of your child.
- Get feedback, through school reports, on teacher insights into your child.
- Encourage the school to avoid making the final year marks of its final year students its major goal.

- Encourage the parent body to review its assessment of what quality education really means.

My suggestions for teachers are:
- Achieve a better balance in the school between the need for control of students and the expression and expansion of individuality.
- Change teacher attitudes to the behavior of students.
- Allow students to express their feelings at school in a 'safe' way.
- Create an environment in which students' opinions are treated as important.
- Allow students a greater input into the school structure and rules.
- Create more fun in the learning process, and particularly commit to accelerated learning methodologies.
- Allow students an opportunity to help each other.
- Create an environment in which abuse or bullying of any description by a teacher is unacceptable.

Before dealing with each of these strategies separately, I will share with you a paper that I prepared and presented in August 1996 to Xavier College's School Liaison Committee in Melbourne. The paper was prepared by me as chairman of a sub-committee of the Liaison Committee, in response to some questions posed by the college principal, Father Michael Stoney. The paper discusses many of the strategies that I am suggesting. I acknowledge the comments and ideas contributed by Michael Tehan. I have edited the paper slightly to exclude particularly confidential, sensitive or irrelevant parts.

Question 1 *What information on school performance would most help parents in the academic guidance of their sons?*

- The assessment and evaluation of each student who enters the college, at any year level, with an immediate reporting to parents of talents, skills, interests, and weaknesses, together with recommended remedial or other action.

- The preparation by the college of a resource kit of remedial programs for as many types of weaknesses as possible, which can be supplied to parents on request or whenever a specific weakness is identified. This resource kit would be compiled from the extraordinarily rich totality of experiences of the Xavier family with remedial programs of any description.

- Early reporting to parents of weaknesses identified in any student, rather than awaiting the regular reporting cycle.

- A process of self-appraisal by each student, which would be supplied to parents with regular reports. This process could include issues such as:
    – How difficult do I find this subject?
    – What has been the most difficult part of life at Xavier this term?
    – What has upset me?

– How much effort do I really feel I have put in over the last term?

– How do I really feel about my achievements in the last term?

– What has been a waste of time at Xavier during the last term?

– What has been the best part of the last term?

– What is the most important thing I have learned about people during the last term?

– What is the most important thing I have learned about myself or my behavior?

- A structured process of teacher appraisal by the students at the end of each term. The problems and challenges raised by this suggestion are many, but Xavier exists for its students. Many parents and students have concerns about giving honest and frank feedback on the negative experiences with particular teachers that have affected them. Disinterest in the student as a consequence of complaints is a real concern, whether justified or not. We consider that one of the most accurate forms of feedback on a teacher's contribution to students is from the students themselves.

   – The process must be wellstructured. Relevant issues for consideration include:

   – Embracing by the teaching staff of the value of student feedback

   – Feedback would not be anonymous

   – Training of students, and maybe parents, in the feedback process would be essential to ensure the integrity of the process

– A commitment by the college that victimization by anyone as a consequence of the process is unacceptable.

– A greater awareness of the commonly occurring problem of teacher–student incompatibility in particular cases, which is not a fault of either party, but simply a fact.

- Reports to include special talents, skills and interests of students that come to the attention of teachers.

Teachers are in a wonderful position to gain insight in rare moments. These insights into a person's talents or interests are important, and must be preserved. (Just imagine the case of a final-year student, lost in career choices, who is able to look through the last eight years of reports (some 24 reports) and refresh his memory of insights that his past teachers have gained into his talents and interests! What a wonderful resource this could be!)

Question 2 *Are children reading enough both within their courses and for general enjoyment? Can parents help to promote more intensive reading habits?*

- Children are not reading enough, and parents can help!
- We recommend that a survey be conducted among all current parents and students to ask them to share the strategies, 'tricks' and experiences they have used or discovered in their own homes to promote reading. The results should be compiled into

a resource kit that would be available on request. The kit would include remedial reading programs that parents have used and found to be valuable.

The reason for the survey is that parents' own experiences are not theoretical. They are real and they are valuable. All parents can benefit from these experiences, and there is no need to constantly reinvent the wheel.

This survey would include all ages of students, including older students, among whom issues of embarrassment because of poor reading skills are much greater than for younger students.

- The writer-in-residence program encourages children to read more. We recommend that this program be continued and expanded.

- In the case of boarders, they miss the opportunities offered by family life to discuss written material. Their general knowledge and understanding of issues is not challenged as it might be in a family situation.

Public issue groups could be established which invite speakers for talks and discussion on issues of interest to boarders, and to which the wider student community could be invited. Expanded discussion would promote a greater interest in and practice of reading.

Question 3 *How can students be encouraged to see their areas of study as worthy of interest for their own sake rather than just as pathways to final-year marks?*

- The college should give powerful support for the guiding philosophy that each student is taught how to find, and is encouraged to find, his unique passion. This would necessarily include a greater knowledge of self.

   As Christ said, 'The kingdom of God is within you.' The college prospectus states that each student will be treated in a way that brings out the unique, and individual, talents that God has given him. This philosophy could be implemented to a more significant degree. The failure to encourage a student's passion, or areas of interest, leads to an attitude that is hardly going to be conducive to study for study's sake.

   We are in support of study for study's sake, and applaud any initiative to reduce the myopia of the final school year process. Unless individual passion is supported and encouraged, the pursuit of individual areas of interest is less likely to occur. One of the most painful experiences for students is to be different, and Xavier can and should reduce the risks to students who wish to be different.

- Increasing the awareness of the negative aspects of parental and peer pressure on the achievement of extraordinary final year results.

   Academic excellence is wonderful, but not at the expense of our souls or our spirits! Australia has the Western world's highest youth suicide rate. Creating an environment that demands school excellence on the one hand, or a life of failure on the other, is hardly conducive to learning for learning's sake, and is considered by health authorities to be a factor in this tragic suicide rate.

- Identifying and encouraging the pursuit of students' special interests will make subjects more enjoyable and relevant to that student. If students can link their unique interests to their subjects, with the help of teachers and the college systems, learning would have a direct and real benefit, rather than the vague and long-term 'benefit' of a good university degree.

  It should also be remembered that Australia has a youth unemployment rate of almost 30 percent, and many of these unemployed people are university graduates. This statistic must be reduced, for we are risking our country's future. By encouraging individual interests, students will be more successful in any given career than those who are in that career simply because they qualified for it through extraordinary VCE results.

  We also recommend that choosing careers by predictions of future 'shortages' in particular professions is a nonsense, and should be discouraged by the college. No one can reliably predict what will happen in the future, and it is misleading to suggest to students that such a process is helpful.

- The *Karpin Report* commissioned by the Australian Government has identified the massive need throughout Australia for future leaders to have far more people skills than is presently the case. These people skills include:
  – negotiating skills

– conflict-resolution skills

– relationship skills

– understanding different personality types

– how to motivate people

– self-awareness.

These skills can be taught, and Xavier is encouraged to take up this challenge. The teaching of such skills will obviously be relevant to students.

- Students should be given greater exposure to vocational training and gain a greater awareness of the benefits to them of learning subjects for learning's sake, rather than learning for the sake of a university degree. One way this can be done is for experts in various fields to speak to the students and share their experiences, and the value to them of learning for learning's sake.

- The college should embrace the concept of cooperative learning, whereby students in all classes help each other on a regular basis during class—that is, the students who learn more quickly help those who require more time. The benefits to teachers and students is profound, and one student's sharing of a love of a subject with another student will be a most positive experience.

Concluding Remarks

The sub-committee acknowledges the challenges raised by many of the above issues.

Each member of the sub-committee is willing to contribute further to expansion of any of the issues, and the implementation of them.

The world is changing, and demands on all of us
are changing. A love of lifetime learning is the greatest
attribute in coping with changing times. Each of the
above suggestions promotes the love of lifetime learning.

Some of the strategies I am advocating are covered by
the paper just quoted. I would like to deal now with those
that are not.

UNDERSTAND THE PHILOSOPHY BEHIND THE SCHOOL'S MISSION STATEMENT

Have you read and considered the mission statement of
your children's school? If so, when was the last time you
read it? Is the mission statement consistent with your views
on life, with what you want for your children? What does
the mission statement mean to you? Are the day-to-day
experiences of your children at school consistent with the
mission statement? If the school is conducted in accordance with the mission statement, will it promote the
accessing of passion by the students?

I was president of the Parents & Friends Association of
St. Roch's Catholic Primary School for five consecutive years.
This is a wonderful, small, local school in Melbourne, where
I have been pleased to send each of my four children. I found
that very few parents had made a conscious decision about
the desired goals and outcomes of the education of their children. At committee meetings of the Association, debates
would begin about particular educational strategies, and
when I considered that they were heading into heated emotional territory, I would ask the parents to consider what they
were seeking for their children before criticizing particular

aspects of the functioning of the school. This suggestion immediately took the heat out of the argument, because the parents realized how few of them had made up their minds on the question, and also realized how different and numerous were the possible goals and outcomes!

As you become clearer on what you want for your children, you will be more effective in ensuring that the school lives up to its mission statement.

DEVELOPING THE UNIQUE ATTRIBUTES OF YOUR CHILD

Most of the highly regarded schools in Melbourne claim in their prospectuses that children will be educated in a way that brings out their unique talents and potential: I am all in favor of that. However, I have spoken to many parents whose children attend these schools and few have been impressed by the *actual* steps taken to promote these unique attributes. As more and more parents request that their children be treated as individuals, the pressure on the school to live up to the statements in their prospectuses will increase, hopefully with concrete results. I am not naive enough to expect this to happen overnight, but I believe that now is the time to begin and continue to increase such requests.

DON'T TREAT FINAL-YEAR MARKS AS THE MAJOR GOAL

In much of the Western world, schools are now a business! They are in the business of attracting new students and keeping existing students, as well as the distasteful process of expelling poor-performing students (or 'encouraging' them to seek other schools). Parents need to choose where to send their children and whether to send them to private or government organizations. I have found that many parents in Australia are greatly influenced by the results achieved by the school's final-year graduates. Thus, the better the results, the greater the number of students. The greater the number of students, the greater the chance of continued funding, and the greater the chance of teachers keeping their jobs.

I understand the pressures that lead to this scenario. I understand the desire of teachers to keep their jobs. However, the price that society, collectively and individually, pays for a myopic view about examination results is too great to ignore. I believe that this myopia makes a major contribution to the level of youth suicide in this country: the pressure that is put on young people to achieve a certain score in their examinations is a nonsense! It is not true that a good final-year examination result is the key to a successful life! I reject any such suggestions, and I encourage all parents to start thinking about their beliefs on this issue.

If schools and teachers change their beliefs about the importance of examination results, then the opportunity is created to let students explore their passion, their interests, their unique perspectives on everything. Let me be clear: I am all in favor of education; after all, it is the business about which I am passionate. However, I say that there is a need to mold the education to fit the child, rather than the current process of molding the child to fit the (in my view, defective) education.

I also admit that I enjoyed my own education, but that was because I excelled at it! It is not hard to enjoy something when you are constantly being praised and encouraged for gaining outstanding results. Looking back to my school days, I now realize that I had no real concern for the students who were struggling, who were rated in the bottom half of the class, and whose experiences at school and the feedback they were given was overwhelmingly negative.

I believe that it is time to change this type of educational philosophy, and I believe that the risks of doing so are minimal. I am convinced that the benefits to the whole community, anywhere in the world, will be extraordinary, for all of the reasons already set out in this book.

WHAT IS QUALITY EDUCATION?

Once you have decided that you want your children to be passionate, that a quality education will encourage such a process rather than hinder it, then changes will need to be instituted. Your fellow parents need to become aware of the issues, and your persistence will help to create that change. Specific steps which can be taken are:

- speak to the chair of the school council about your concerns
- speak to your fellow parents
- put the issue onto the agenda papers at parent meetings: most parent meetings of which I am aware discuss fundraising issues, so your interest and commitment will be a welcome change

- speak to teachers with whom you have some rapport
- buy a copy of this book and give it to other parents!

BALANCE 'NEED FOR CONTROL' WITH INDIVIDUALITY

Teachers need to control students. An uncontrolled classroom will hinder learning, will hamper those students who are doing what they enjoy in the current environment. But too much control by the teacher, excessively rigid methods of teaching, will squash spirit and intuition and motivation.

My thoughts on education have been influenced by a paper entitled 'Confederacy of Dunces: The Tyranny of Compulsory Schooling' by John Taylor Gatto, a teacher of 26 years' experience who was once named New York State Teacher of the Year. The paper is the text of a speech he delivered in the early 1990s at the University of Texas in Austin. The gist of the paper is contained in the following paragraphs:

> Modern scientific stupidity masquerades as intellectual knowledge—which it is not. Real knowledge is earned only by ceaseless questioning of yourself and others, and by the labor of independent verification; you can't buy it from a government agent, a social worker, a psychologist, a licensed specialist, or a schoolteacher. There isn't a public school in the country set up to allow the discovery of real knowledge—not even the best one—although here and there individual teachers, like guerilla fighters, sabotage the system and work towards this ideal. But since schools are

set up to classify people rather than to see them as unique, even the best schoolteachers are strictly limited in the amount of questioning they can tolerate.

The new dumbness—the non-thought of received ideas—is much more dangerous than simple ignorance, because it is really about thought control. In school, a washing away of the innate power of individual mind takes place, a 'cleansing' so comprehensive that original thinking becomes difficult. If you do not believe this development was part of the intentional design of schooling, you should read William Torrey Harris' *The Philosophy of Education*. Harris was the U.S. Commissioner of Education at the turn of the century and the man most influential in standardizing our schools. Listen to the man.

'99 (students) out of a 100,' writes Harris, 'are automata, careful to walk in the prescribed paths, careful to follow the prescribed custom.' This is not an accident, Harris explains, but the 'result of substantial education, which, scientifically defined, is the subsumption of the individual.'

Scientific education subsumes the individual until his or her behaviour becomes robotic. Those are the thoughts of the most influential U.S. Commissioner of Education we have had so far.

The great theological scholar Dietrich Bonhoeffer raised this issue of the new dumbness in his brilliant analysis of Nazism, in which he sought to comprehend how the best-schooled nation in the world, Germany, could fall under its sway. He concluded that Nazism could be understood *only* as the psychological product of good schooling. The sheer weight of received ideas, pre-thought thoughts, was so overwhelming that individuals gave up trying to assess things for themselves. Why struggle to invent a map of the world or of the human conscience when schools and media offer thousands of ready-made maps, pre-thought thoughts?

The new dumbness is particularly deadly to middle- and upper-middle class people, who have already been made shallow by the multiple requirements to conform. Too many people, uneasily convinced that they must know something because of a degree, diploma, or license, remain so convinced until a brutal divorce, alienation from their children, loss of employment, or periodic fits of meaninglessness manage to tip the precarious mental balance of their incomplete humanity, their stillborn adult lives.

Gatto summarizes well the price we pay, as human beings, for too much control. How much is too much? That depends on the unique classes that your children are part of, and the unique teacher that is teaching that class! Unless you take an interest in the issue, you will not be able to influence any changes. Why would you take an interest? My answer is 'because your children's future depends on it.'

CHANGE TEACHER ATTITUDES TO THE BEHAVIOR OF STUDENTS

As the education system presently stands, and having regard to the present basis on which teachers and schools are assessed, there are few benefits for teachers in changing their own behavior and attitudes. Unless parents change *their* attitudes, teachers will not do so.

Now this book is not intended to be a 'teacher bashing' exercise. Teachers are responding to the existing system: they did not create it. Parents are the key 'clients' of the education 'business,' and teachers will change when their 'clients' demand it. Each one of us who is a parent must take responsibility for the way in which our children are educated, the way they are treated by their schools and teachers, and we must understand that positive changes are unlikely unless we take action.

ALLOW STUDENTS TO EXPRESS THEIR FEELINGS AT SCHOOL IN A 'SAFE' WAY

Each student is unique. They have unique feelings. They do not, in most cases, understand that their feelings are unique: conformity leads to harmony, uniqueness often leads to students being rejected, ostracized, or bullied.

It is possible to create an environment at school where 'safe' opportunities are created for *all and any* students to express what they are feeling. Our feelings are the primary information source for our passion, for our spirit: to deny our feelings is to deny our true selves. I believe that teachers have sufficient training to handle the expression of feelings, but they will not change the system and create the necessary new structures unless parents demand the changes. Leaving such matters to governments is a total abdication of parental responsibility! Therefore, consider demanding change.

CREATE AN ENVIRONMENT IN WHICH STUDENTS' OPINIONS MATTER

Do your children feel important and valued in the school environment? Have you asked them this question? Are their opinions valued by the teachers?

Each time our children's opinions are discounted, their uniqueness, their independent thinking, indeed their thinking itself, is squashed. It is no surprise that students who complete school do not know what they want to do, because their individual choices, preferences and opinions have been ignored for years.

We would gain great gifts of insight and wisdom if we listened to our children in school. They often know better than the teachers what is really going on. Unless we listen to them, that insight and that wisdom are lost, and a distrust of our intuitive wisdom is fostered. No wonder finding our passion is difficult, after years of such invalidation.

ENCOURAGE STUDENT INPUT INTO THE SCHOOL STRUCTURE AND RULES

This strategy is similar to a number of the preceding strategies, so I simply suggest that student wisdom and insight can and should be more effectively harnessed.

CREATE MORE FUN IN THE LEARNING PROCESS

The science of Neurolinguistic Programming has taught us many things about how human beings learn. Accelerated learning methodologies use this science to create an environment in which different students are catered for, where different learning styles are accommodated by the school.

The most useful book that I have read on this topic is Bobbi De Porter's classic *Quantum Learning: Unleashing the Genius in You*. The book's important message is contained on its back cover: 'Take control of your life...free your natural genius to perform to its true potential.' *Quantum Learning* features a revolutionary new format that introduces the reader to a world of learning unlike any other:

> Never before has a guide been designed to accommodate the unique learning style of the individual. Whether you are a professional, a student, or a person who simply wants to improve his or her learning capacity, this extraordinary guide will increase your personal power, help you learn more, earn more...and take you where you want to go.

I commend the book to you, to your children, and to their teachers.

ALLOW STUDENTS A GREATER OPPORTUNITY TO HELP EACH OTHER

Teachers are under enormous pressure today. Their jobs are often at risk, and like the rest of the workforce, long-term job security is a thing of the past.

Teachers are generally motivated to generate good results, and are generally concerned about the welfare of students. However, they often fail to communicate their message to particular students. These are the times when using fellow students to help each other is a simple solution to a complex problem. And yet, I have not experienced or heard of many teachers using this strategy.

My daughter, Rebecca, in year eight, was a very successful German-language student. I encouraged her teacher to use Rebecca's skills with fellow students. She did so, with wonderful results. Up to that time, Rebecca was usually finishing tasks early and becoming bored. When the teacher allowed other students to use her skills, they were keen to do so, and the communication between Rebecca and her colleagues was in many instances better than between teacher and student. This is not because of any failure on the teacher's part, but because the student's learning methodology or modality was more easily accessed by Rebecca. Overworked teachers should be using students who understand particular issues to help other students who do not understand them.

I have practiced this strategy with adult learning to great effect. When I attended the Hawaiian Business School in 1993, one day of the course was devoted to business accounting. The facilitator was an accountant, and exercises were handed to the 151 participants. All participants were encouraged to help any other participant as soon as the exercises were complete. Since I'd been a tax/business lawyer for years, and understood balance sheets and accounting concepts, I finished very quickly and was able to spend long periods of time helping others on a one-on-one basis, ensuring that they really understood what they were doing. I gained from explaining the concepts, the other participant learned the lesson, I did not get bored, and the facilitator did not become frustrated by the different rates of learning and understanding in a large group of people.

Overall, I recommend the use of such a process in any educational environment. I am not aware of any pitfalls in it, other than the bruised egos of certain types of people!

DECRY ANY ABUSE BY A TEACHER

Teachers can abuse students in a variety of ways. My children have found the most common and the most insidious abuse to be when teachers criticize students for their poor performance, often resulting in those students feeling inferior and 'not good enough.'

Such behavior should not be accepted, and I doubt that any school principal would disagree. However, the abuse happens, and you will find out about it only if you are practicing your communication with your children. Ask them what happens when students make mistakes. Ask them what happens when certain students work more slowly than others. Explore the detail, and invest the time to do so.

In year four, my young son Timothy was being taught by a relieving teacher at St. Roch's. Tim is always keen to do the right thing, and often too keen for his own good. He beats himself up whenever he makes a mistake, and therefore will try hard to avoid making them. I constantly reinforce to him that the more he makes mistakes, the quicker he is learning. One day, Tim was asked to read a passage aloud to the class. He made a number of pronunciation errors, and the teacher encouraged the other students to laugh at Tim. He was mortified. Jenny and I learned of the experience from Nicholas, Tim's twin brother, who was in the same class.

It was clear that the teacher's strategy was to create motivation to improve learning by creating pain and embarrassment whenever mistakes were made. We immediately went to see the principal, who understood and shared our concern. The problem was addressed in this particular case, but I have no doubt that many teachers still attempt to motivate students through fear of being embarrassed and laughed at for errors. Such behavior, in my view, is abuse, or bullying, and must be stopped. Abuse for mistakes is a squashing of the spirit, a squashing of passion, and is a sure way to blocks an attitude that supports a love of learning.

KEY POINTS FOR CHAPTER 9

- Review the subheads in this chapter.
- Parents can significantly influence the value of school to their children.
- Success in life is not primarily dependent on school examination results.
- Decide what you want your children to gain from their school experience.
- Encourage your children to think for themselves.
- Encourage cooperative learning among students at school.
- Do not allow students to be laughed at or humiliated for their mistakes.

CHAPTER 10
Anyway

CHAPTER 10
Anyway

'*Unless we try to do something beyond what we have alredy mastered we cannot grow.*'

— **Ronald Osborn**

*I*n my Time Manager, which I have been carrying with me for many years, I have been including inspirational quotes and thoughts. Whenever it is necessary to wait, I turn to these thoughts to remind me of perspectives that can easily be forgotten. The pleasure I receive from the reminders far outweighs the pain of waiting!

By way of concluding this book, I would like to share one of these 'gems' with you, entitled *Anyway*:

People are unreasonable, illogical, and self-centered.
Love them anyway!
If you do good, people will accuse you of selfish ulterior
  motives.
Do good anyway!

Passionate People Produce

*If you are successful, you will win false friends and
   true enemies.*
Succeed anyway!
The good you do today will be forgotten tomorrow.
Do good anyway!
Honesty and frankness make you vulnerable.
Be honest and frank anyway!
*The biggest person with the biggest ideas can be shot
   down by the smallest people with the smallest minds.*
Think big anyway!
People favor underdogs but follow only top dogs.
Fight for some underdogs anyway!
*What you spend years building may be destroyed
   overnight.*
Build anyway!
*People really need help, but may attack you if you
   help them.*
Help people anyway!
*Give the world the best you have and you'll get kicked
   in the teeth.*
Give the world the best you've got anyway!
   (Author Unknown)

I have taken the liberty of adding a postscript to this
inspirational piece:
*If you are passionate in your life, people will be
   jealous and will criticize you*
Be passionate anyway!

EPILOGUE

I used to *believe* that writing a book is difficult. Now, having completed one, I *know* that it is difficult! There has been more pain than pleasure during the writing process, but the pleasure I now feel in having completed the task more than compensates for the pain.

That is the equation that faces you when deciding whether to discover, and to pursue, your passion in your unique humanness. Pain and risk will be involved, but pleasure and reward will follow. Your passion makes you capable of extraordinary achievement, and pursuing it will ensure that you discover, and then fulfill, your life's purpose.

All that remains now is for you to choose....

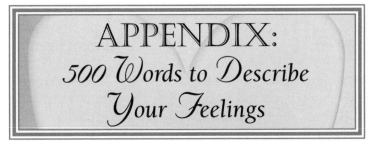

APPENDIX:
500 Words to Describe Your Feelings

The words listed below have been extracted primarily from the *Shorter Oxford English Dictionary*. They describe states of feeling and emotion. They are listed to increase your awareness of the possible range of your feelings and the fine distinctions between them. Making those distinctions is usually difficult if you want to describe *exactly* what you are feeling. As usual, 'practice makes better'!

ABASHED	ALIVE	BAD
ABHOR	AMAZING	BAFFLED
ABLE	AMIABLE	BANAL
ABSURD	AMICABLE	BASHFUL
ABUNDANT	AMUSING	BENEFICIAL
ABUSIVE	ANGRY	BENEVOLENCE
ACCOMMODATING	ANTAGONISTIC	BEST
ACCOMPLISHMENT	ANXIOUS	BETTER
ACHIEVEMENT	APATHETIC	BEWILDERED
ACTIVE	APPALLING	BITING
ADEPT	APPREHENSIVE	BITTER
ADEQUATE	APT	BIZARRE
ADMIRABLE	ARDENT	BLAMELESS
ADROITNESS	ASSURED	BLITHE
ADVANTAGEOUS	ASTONISHING	BLOSSOM
ADVENTUROUS	ASTOUNDING	BLUNT
ADVERSE	ASTRINGENT	BLUSHING
AFFECTIONATE	ASTUTE	BOLD
AFRAID	AUDACIOUS	BORING
AGHAST	AUSPICIOUS	BOUNTIFUL
AGITATED	AVERSE	BRAVE
AGREEABLE	AWFUL	BRIGHT

BRILLIANT	CONVIVIAL	DISTINGUISHED
BURNING	COOL	DISTRAUGHT
BUSTLING	COPIOUS	DISTURBED
CALM	CORDIAL	DOCILE
CANDID	CORRUPT	DOUBTFUL
CAPABLE	COURAGEOUS	DOWNHEARTED
CAPRICIOUS	COURTEOUS	DRAB
CATASTROPHIC	COWARDLY	DREADFUL
CHARITABLE	COY	DROLL
CHARMING	CRAZY	DULL
CHEERFUL	CUTTING	DUMB
CHIVALROUS	CYNICAL	DUTIFUL
CIVILIZED	DAPPER	DYNAMIC
CLASHING	DARING	EAGER
CLEVER	DARK	EARNEST
COLORLESS	DEATHLY	ECCENTRIC
COMFORTABLE	DECEITFUL	EFFERVESCENT
COMICAL	DEFECTIVE	EFFICIENT
COMMENDABLE	DEFERENTIAL	ELATED
COMPASSIONATE	DEFIANT	EMINENCE
COMPETENT	DEJECTED	EMOTIONAL
COMPETITIVE	DELICATE	ENCHANTING
COMPLACENT	DELIGHT	ENERGETIC
COMPLETE	DEMURE	ENRAGED
COMPOSED	DEPRESSED	ENTERTAINING
CONCERNED	DERANGED	ENTHUSIASTIC
CONFIDENT	DESIRE	EQUITABLE
CONFLICTING	DETERMINED	EQUIVOCAL
CONFOUNDED	DETESTABLE	ERRATIC
CONFRONTING	DEVOTED	ESSENTIAL
CONFUSED	DIM	ETHICAL
CONGENIAL	DIRE	EVIL
CONSCIENTIOUS	DISAGREEABLE	EXCELLENT
CONSENT	DISASTROUS	EXCEPTIONAL
CONSIDERATE	DISGRACEFUL	EXEMPLARY
CONTENTED	DISGUSTED	EXHILARATED
CONTRADICTORY	DISMAL	EXTRAORDINARY
CONTRARY	DISPIRITED	EXUBERANT

FABULOUS	FURIOUS	HUMANE
FACETIOUS	GALLANT	HUMBLE
FACILE	GAME	HUMOROUS
FAILURE	GAY	HURTFUL
FAIR	GENEROUS	HYPOCRITICAL
FAITHFUL	GENIAL	IMPAIRED
FAMILIAR	GENTLE	IMPERFECT
FANTASTIC	GENUINE	IMPERTINENT
FATIGUE	GHASTLY	IMPRESSED
FATUOUS	GIFTED	IMPRESSIVE
FAVORABLE	GLAD	IMPUDENT
FEARFUL	GLEAMING	INADEQUATE
FEARLESS	GLEEFUL	INANE
FEEBLE	GLOOMY	INCENSED
FEROCIOUS	GLOWING	INCLEMENT
FERVENT	GOOD	INCOMPLETE
FESTIVE	GRACIOUS	INCREDIBLE
FLIMSY	GRAND	INDULGENT
FLIPPANT	GRATIFIED	INFATUATED
FLUSTERED	GRAVE	INSANE
FOCUSED	GRIM	INSIPID
FOOLISH	GRISLY	INSULTING
FORCEFUL	GRUESOME	INTELLIGENT
FORGIVING	HAPPY	INTENSE
FORLORN	HARMONY	INTERESTING
FORTHRIGHT	HATEFUL	INTIMATE
FORTUNATE	HEALTHY	INTOLERABLE
FRAGILE	HEARTY	INTREPID
FRAIL	HEATED	INVENTIVE
FRANK	HELPFUL	IRATE
FRANTIC	HIDEOUS	JOCULAR
FREE	HONEST	JOVIAL
FRIENDLY	HONORABLE	JOY
FRIGHTFUL	HOPELESS	JOYOUS
FRIVOLOUS	HORRIBLE	JUST
FROLICSOME	HORRID	KEEN
FULFILLMENT	HORRIFIED	KINDNESS
FUNNY	HOSTILE	LAVISH

LIKE	OFFENSIVE	PROSPERITY
LOVE	OPEN	PROSPEROUS
LOYALTY	OPPOSING	PRUDISH
LUCKY	OUTLANDISH	QUALIFIED
LUDICROUS	OUTRAGEOUS	QUICK
LUSTROUS	OUTSPOKEN	RADIANT
MAD	OVERWHELMED	RADICAL
MAGNIFICENT	PAINFUL	RAGING
MANNERLY	PANICKY	REAL
MARVELOUS	PASSIONATE	REFINED
MASTER	PENETRATING	REJOICE
MELANCHOLY	PERCEPTIVE	REMARKABLE
MERCIFUL	PERPLEXED	RESISTING
MERIT	PERSPICACIOUS	RESPECTFUL
MERRY	PESSIMISTIC	RESPONSIBLE
MIGHTY	PETTY	RESPONSIVE
MILD	PHENOMENAL	RETALIATION
MISERABLE	PIOUS	RETIRING
MODERATE	PITIFUL	REVENGEFUL
MODEST	PLAYFUL	REVERENTIAL
MONOTONOUS	PLEASANT	RIDICULOUS
MONSTROUS	PLEASED	RIGHTEOUS
MORAL	PLEASING	ROBUST
MOROSE	PLEASURE	ROTTEN
MOURNFUL	POIGNANT	RUEFUL
MOVED	POLITE	RUINED
MYSTIFIED	POOR	SAD
NASTY	PORTENTOUS	SAGACIOUS
NAUGHTY	POTENT	SATISFACTORY
NEGATIVE	POWERFUL	SECURE
NEIGHBORLY	PRACTICAL	SEDATE
NERVOUS	PRAISEWORTHY	SENSATIONAL
NOBLE	PRIGGISH	SENSELESS
OBEDIENT	PROFICIENCY	SENSIBLE
OBLIGING	PROFITABLE	SERIOUS
OBSCURE	PROMISING	SEVERE
ODD	PROPER	SHAKEN
OFFENDED	PROSAIC	SHAMEFUL

SHARP
SHINING
SHOCKING
SHREWD
SHY
SILENT
SILLY
SINCERE
SINISTER
SKILLED
SMART
SOCIABLE
SOLEMN
SOMBER
SORROWFUL
SORRY
SOUR
SPARKLING
SPECTACULAR
SPEECHLESS
SPIRITED
SPLENDID
SPONTANEOUS
STAID
STALWART
STRENUOUS
STRONG
STUPID
STURDY
SUBMISSIVE
SUCCESS
SULLEN
SUPERB
SUPERFICIAL
SUPERIOR
SURE
SURPRISING
SYMPATHETIC

TAINTED
TALENTED
TAME
TEDIOUS
TEEMING
TENDER
TERRIFIED
THRIVE
TIMID
TIMOROUS
TIRED
TOUCHING
TRAGIC
TRANQUIL
TRAUMATIC
TREMULOUS
TRIFLING
TRIVIAL
TROUBLED
TRUSTED
TRUTHFUL
UNASSUMING
UNBELIEVABLE
UNFAVORABLE
UNFRIENDLY
UNSATISFACTORY
UNUSUAL
UPSET
USEFUL
VAGUE
VICIOUS
VIGOROUS
VILE
VINDICTIVE
VIOLENT
VIRTUE
VITAL
VIVACIOUS

VIVID
WARM
WEAK
WHIMSICAL
WICKED
WILD
WILLFUL
WITLESS
WITTY
WOBBLY
WONDERFUL
WORTHLESS
WRATHFUL
WRONG
ZEALOUS

FURTHER READING

I have read each of the books below: they comprise a treasured portion of my much-loved library. The information and the insights contained in the books gave me valuable learning experiences which continue to play a part in my daily life.

In preparing this listing, I chose not to distinguish between books that are referred to in the text and those that are not. However, all books that have been referred to in the text are listed.

Baldwin, J. (1996) *Bucky Works*. New York: John Wiley & Sons, Inc.

Bernard, Michael E (1997) *You Can Do It! for parents*. Australia: Wilkinson Books.

Biddulph, Steve (1994) *Manhood*. Australia: Finch Publishing.

Brown, Barbara B (1980) *Super-Mind The Ultimate Energy*. New York: Harper & Row.

Carnegie, Roderick M & Butlin, Matthew (1993) *Managing the Innovating Enterprise*. Australia: The Business Library and the Business Council of Australia.

Carey, Ken (1988) *Return of the Bird Tribes*. New York: HarperCollins Publishers.

Chopra, Deepak (1993) *Ageless Body, Timeless Mind*. New York: Harmony Books.

Chopra, Deepak (1989) *Quantum Healing*. New York: Bantam Books.

Chu, Chin-Ning (1995) *Thick Face, Black Heart*.
New York: AMC Publishing

Clason, George S. (1955) *The Richest Man in Babylon*.
New York: Bantam Books

Covey, Stephen R. (1989) *The 7 Habits of Highly Effective People*. New York: Simon & Schuster.

DeBono, Edward (1990) *I Am Right, You Are Wrong*.
Australia: Penguin Books

De Geus, Arie *The Living Company*

Demartini, John F. (1997) *Count Your Blessings*.
Australia: Element Books, Inc.

DeMello, Anthony (1990) *Awareness*. London: Fount Paperbacks.

DePorter, Bobbi with Hernacki, Mike (1992) *Quantum Learning*. New York: Dell Publishing.

Diamond, Harvey & Marilyn (1985) *Fit For Life*.
New York: Warner Books.

Dyer, Wayne W. (1995) *Your Sacred Self*. Australia: HarperCollins Publishers.

Edmondson, Amy C. (1992) *A Fuller Explanation*.
New York: Van Nostrand Reinhold.

Fuller, R. Buckminster (1992) *Cosmography*. New York: Macmillan Publishing.

Fuller, R. Buckminster (1981) *Critical Path*. New York: St Martin's Press.

Fuller, R. Buckminster (1971) *Operating Manual for Spaceship Earth*. USA: Penguin Group

Gerber, Michael E. (1986) *The E Myth*. USA: Harper Business

Gibran, Kahlil (1970) *The Prophet*. London: Heinemann.

Goleman, Daniel (1996) *Emotional Intelligence.*
Great Britain: Bloomsbury Publishing.

Handy, Charles (1995) *The Empty Raincoat.*
Great Britain: Arrow Books.

Hill, Napoleon (1966) *Think & Grow Rich.* Canada:
Wilshire Books.

Honderich, Ted (ed.) (1995) *The Oxford Companion to
Philosophy.* New York: Oxford University Press.

Jampolsky, Gerald G. (1979) *Love Is Letting Go of Fear.*
USA: Celestial Arts.

Karpin, David S. & others (1995) *Enterprising Nation.
Renewing Australia's Managers to meet the challenges
of the Asia-Pacific Century. Report of the Industry
Task Force on Leadership and Management Skills.*
Australian Government Publishing Service.

Katzenbach, Jon R., & Smith, Douglas K (1993) *The
Wisdom of Teams.* USA: McKinsey & Co.

Keen, Sam (1992) *The Passionate Life.* New York:
HarperCollins Publishers.

Kiyosaki, Robert T. (1991) *If You Want to Be Rich &
Happy, Don't Go to School?* California: The
Excellerated Learning Institute.

Maltz, Maxwell (1969) *Psycho-Cybernetics.* USA:
Prentice-Hall

Moore, Thomas (1992) *Care of the Soul.* New York:
Harper Perennial.

Nacson, Leon (1993) *A Dreamer's Guide to the Galaxy.*
NSW: Leon Nacson

Ostrander, Sheila (1979) *Super Learning.* New York:
Souvenir Press.

Peters, Thomas J and Austin, Nancy K (1985) *A Passion for Excellence*. New York: Random House.

Prior, Tom (1995) *Sheeds, A Touch of Cunning*. Melbourne: Wilkinson Books.

Reanney, Darryl (1991) *The Death of Forever*. Melbourne: Longman Cheshire.

Reanney, Darryl (1994) *Music of the Mind*. Victoria: Hill of Content Publishing Co.

Redfield, James (1993) *The Celestine Prophecy*. USA: Bantam Books.

Reilly, Graham (Ed) (1995) *My First Love & Turning Points*. Victoria: Julie Morgan Marketing

Robbins, Anthony (1991) *Awaken the Giant Within*. New York: Simon & Schuster.

Robbins, Anthony (1989) *Unlimited Power*. New York: Simon & Schuster.

Rose, Colin (1991) *Accelerated Learning*. Great Britain: Accelerated Learning Systems.

Silva, Jose (1989) *The Silva Mind Control Method*. New York: Pocket Books.

Sinetar, Marsha (1987) *Do What You Love and the Money Will Follow*. New York: Dell Publishing.

Stynes, Jim (1995) *Whatever it Takes*. Australia: Celebrity Publishing.

Walsch, Neale D. (1995) *Conversations with God*. NSW: Hodder & Stoughton.

Whyte, David (1994) *The Heart Aroused*. New York: Dell Publishing.

Williamson, Marianne (1992) *A Return to Love*. New York: HarperCollins.

BIOGRAPHICAL NOTES

CHARLES KOVESS graduated from the University of Melbourne with a Bachelor of Laws with Honors in 1973, and gained his Master of Laws from Monash University in 1980. He practiced business and taxation law passionately and successfully for 20 years.

Charles left the law in June 1993 to pursue his passion for increasing passion! He believes that accessing and harnessing their passion is the fundamental key to business success in these changing and challenging times. In March 2001, Charles earned the coveted 'Certified Speaking Professional' accreditation, the highest international qualification for speaking professionals.

Graduating from the Business School for Entrepreneurs in Hawaii, co-facilitated by Robert Kyosaki, and completing the ELI Super Teaching Course in August 1993, reinforced the accelerated learning methodologies that Charles uses in his keynote presentations, seminar and workshop programs.

Clients to whom he has presented include Deakin Australia, ANZ Banking Group, Tourism Victoria, Commonwealth Bank of Australia, National Australia Bank, Optus, Essendon Football Club, Brisbane Lions Football Club, Telstra, AXA (formerly National Mutual), Federal Government's Department of Finance &

Administration, Victorian Government's Department of Treasury & Finance, Australia Post, Colonial State Bank, and Uncle Ben's.

Among a lifetime of voluntary positions in which Charles has made significant contributions, he is President of the Australia-Hungary Chamber of Commerce (his 11th year), trustee of Global Energy Network Inc, President of the National Speakers' Association of Australia (Victorian Chapter), former Board Member of Save the Children Victoria, former Councillor of the Law Institute of Victoria, and former Chairman of the EC Chambers of Commerce & Industry (Vic.) Inc.

Charles is not only passionate about business: he loves sport. He has competed for 18 consecutive seasons in triathlons, he has completed the Ironman Triathlon, he has run eight marathons, and he is an internationally qualified water polo referee. He is the father of four children.

His second book, *Passionate Performance*, was released in March of 2000.

INDEX

NOTES

NOTES

NOTES

We hope you enjoyed this Hay House book.
If you'd like to receive a free catalog featuring additional
Hay House books and products, or if you'd like information about
the Hay Foundation, please contact:

Hay House, Inc.
P.O. Box 5100
Carlsbad, CA 92018-5100

(760) 431-7695 or **(800) 654-5126**
(760) 431-6948 (fax) or **(800) 650-5115 (fax)**
www.hayhouse.com

* * *

Published and distributed in Australia by:
Hay House Australia Pty. Ltd. • 18/36 Ralph St. • Alexandria NSW 2015 •
Phone: 612-9669-4299 • *Fax:* 612-9669-4144 • www.hayhouse.com.au

Published and distributed in the United Kingdom by:
Hay House UK, Ltd. • Unit 62, Canalot Studios •
222 Kensal Rd., London W10 5BN • *Phone:* 44-20-8962-1230 •
Fax: 44-20-8962-1239 • www.hayhouse.co.uk

Published and distributed in the Republic of South Africa by:
Hay House SA (Pty), Ltd., P.O. Box 990, Witkoppen 2068 •
Phone/Fax: 2711-7012233 • orders@psdprom.co.za

Distributed in Canada by:
Raincoast • 9050 Shaughnessy St., Vancouver, B.C. V6P 6E5 •
Phone: (604) 323-7100 • *Fax:* (604) 323-2600

Sign up via the Hay House USA Website to receive the Hay House
online newsletter and stay informed about what's going on with your
favorite authors. You'll receive bimonthly announcements about:
Discounts and Offers, Special Events, Product Highlights,
Free Excerpts, Giveaways, and more!
www.hayhouse.com